Aptitude for Destruction

Volume 1: Organizational Learning in Terrorist Groups and Its Implications for Combating Terrorism

Brian A. Jackson

with
John C. Baker
Kim Cragin
John Parachini
Horacio R. Trujillo
Peter Chalk

Prepared for the National Institute of Justice

INFRASTRUCTURE, SAFETY,
AND ENVIRONMENT

The research described in this report was supported by Grant No. 2003-IJ-CX-1022 awarded by the National Institute of Justice, Office of Justice Programs, U.S. Department of Justice. The research was conducted within RAND Infrastructure, Safety, and Environment (ISE), a division of the RAND Corporation, for the National Institute of Justice. Points of view in this document are those of the authors and do not necessarily represent the official position or policies of the U.S. Department of Justice.

Library of Congress Cataloging-in-Publication Data

Aptitude for destruction : organizational learning in terrorist groups and its implications for combating terrorism / Brian A. Jackson ... [et al.].
    p. cm.
    "MG-331."
    Includes bibliographical references.
    ISBN 0-8330-3764-1 (pbk. : alk. paper)
    1. Terrorists. 2. Organizational learning. 3. Terrorism—Prevention—Government policy. I. Jackson, Brian A. (Brian Anthony) II.Title.

HV6431.A67 2005
303.6'25—dc22
                                                              2005003983

Photo courtesy of iStockphoto.com Inc. Copyright 2005 iStockphoto Inc.
Online at http://www.iStockphoto.com

The RAND Corporation is a nonprofit research organization providing objective analysis and effective solutions that address the challenges facing the public and private sectors around the world. RAND's publications do not necessarily reflect the opinions of its research clients and sponsors.

RAND® is a registered trademark.

Cover design by Stephen Bloodsworth

© Copyright 2005 RAND Corporation

Published 2005 by the RAND Corporation
1776 Main Street, P.O. Box 2138, Santa Monica, CA 90407-2138
1200 South Hayes Street, Arlington, VA 22202-5050
201 North Craig Street, Suite 202, Pittsburgh, PA 15213-1516
RAND URL: http://www.rand.org/
To order RAND documents or to obtain additional information, contact
Distribution Services: Telephone: (310) 451-7002;
Fax: (310) 451-6915; Email: order@rand.org

Preface

Continuing conflicts between violent groups and states generate an ever-present demand for higher quality and more timely information to support operations to combat terrorism. In particular, better ways are needed to understand how terrorist and insurgent groups adapt over time into more-effective organizations and increasingly dangerous threats. To adapt, terrorist organizations must learn. A group's ability to learn determines its chance of success, since learning is the link between what the group wants to do and its ability to gather the needed information and resources to actually do it. Despite the importance of terrorist group learning, comparatively little focused research effort has been directed at understanding this process and identifying the factors that influence group learning ability. While relevant data and insights can be found in the literature on terrorism and terrorist organizations, this information has not been collected and systematically analyzed to assess its importance from the perspective of efforts to combat terrorism. This study addresses that need in an effort to both analyze current understanding and stimulate further study and research in this area.

The National Institute of Justice provided funding to the RAND Corporation to conduct an analysis of organizational learning in terrorist groups and assess its implications for efforts to combat terrorism. The work was performed between November 2003 and November 2004, a period during which the threat of international terrorism was high and concern about the capabilities of terrorist organizations and how they might change over time was a central focus of policy debate and U.S. homeland security planning. The study is described in this report and in a companion volume, *Aptitude for Destruction, Volume 2: Case Studies of Organizational Learning in Five Terrorist Groups*-332-NIJ, which examines the innovation and learning activities of five groups selected to represent the spectrum of organizations that have used terrorist tactics.

This report should be of interest to a wide range of audiences, including professionals with interests in terrorism, counterterrorism, emergency response planning, and homeland security. It extends RAND's ongoing research on terrorism and domestic security issues. Related RAND publications include the following:

- Brian A. Jackson et al., *Aptitude for Destruction, Volume 2: Case Studies of Organizational Learning in Five Terrorist Groups*, MG-332-NIJ, 2005.
- Brian A. Jackson et al., *Protecting Emergency Responders: Lessons Learned from Terrorist Attacks*, CF-176-OSTP, 2002.
- Kim Cragin and Sara A. Daly, *The Dynamic Terrorist Threat: An Assessment of Group Motivations and Capabilities in a Changing World*, MR-1782-AF, 2004.
- Peter Chalk and William Rosenau, *Confronting the "Enemy Within": Security Intelligence, the Police, and Counterterrorism in Four Democracies*, MG-100-RC, 2004.
- Bruce Hoffman, *Insurgency and Counterinsurgency in Iraq*, OP-127-IPC/CMEPP, 2004.

This research was conducted within RAND Infrastructure, Safety, and Environment (ISE), a division of the RAND Corporation. The mission of RAND ISE is to improve the development, operation, use, and protection of society's essential built and natural assets; and to enhance the related social assets of safety and security of individuals in transit and in their workplaces and communities. The ISE research portfolio encompasses research and analysis on a broad range of policy areas including homeland security, criminal justice, public safety, occupational safety, the environment, energy, natural resources, climate, agriculture, economic development, transportation, information and telecommunications technologies, space exploration, and other aspects of science and technology policy. Inquiries regarding RAND Infrastructure, Safety, and Environment may be directed to

Debra Knopman, Vice President and Director
RAND Infrastructure, Safety, and Environment
1200 South Hayes Street
Arlington, Virginia 22202
703-413-1100
Email: ise@rand.org
http://www.rand.org/ise

Contents

Figures

Summary

If a terrorist group lacks the ability to learn, its effectiveness in achieving its goals will largely be determined by chance—the chance that its members already have the necessary skills to carry out operations and support activities; the chance that its current tactics are effective against desirable targets and against current antiterrorism measures; and the chance that shifts made by the group will prove to be beneficial.[1] Similarly, in a dynamic environment, a terrorist organization that cannot learn will not be able to effectively adapt to new developments in intelligence gathering and law enforcement.

But when a terrorist group can learn—and learn well—it can act systematically to fulfill its needs, strengthen its capabilities, and advance its strategic agenda. The ability to learn allows a terrorist group to purposefully adapt to ever-evolving circumstances by

- Developing, improving, and employing new weapons or tactics that can enable it to change its capabilities over time
- Improving its members' skills in applying current weapons or tactics
- Collecting and utilizing the intelligence information needed to mount operations effectively
- Thwarting countermeasures and improve its chance of surviving attempts to destroy it
- Preserving the capabilities it has developed even if some of its members are lost

---

[1] While change in the way a group carries out its activities is frequently indicative of learning, the occurrence of change is not sufficient to indicate that organizational learning has occurred. Changes are not necessarily intentional; they can be made unintentionally or for exogenous reasons incidental to the behavior that is changed (e.g., a change may occur in one area simply as a result of a change made in another). In this study, we define learning as sustained changes that involve intentional action by or within a group at some point—such as one or more of the following: intentional seeking of new knowledge or new ways or doing things; intentional evaluation of behaviors, new or old, that leads to efforts to retain valuable behaviors and discard others; and/or intentional dissemination of knowledge within a group or among groups when such knowledge is deemed useful or beneficial. Furthermore, we categorize as learning only changes that are beneficial to the terrorist group.

A terrorist group's ability to learn is therefore a primary determinant of the level of threat it poses, since learning is the route through which organizations can seek solutions to the problems that bound their freedom of action and limit their ability to pursue their goals in changing operational and security circumstances.

The Need to Understand Organizational Learning

Discerning how terrorist groups learn in a dynamic environment is crucial for understanding terrorism. With increased understanding of group learning processes, intelligence analysts and security planners will be better able to

- **Assess the level of threat posed by a terrorist organization,** which can be radically altered by effective learning.
- **Design and implement strategies for combating terrorism,** using knowledge of how terrorist groups use learning to blunt or overcome the countermeasures and security systems intended to defeat their efforts.
- **Appropriately allocate resources for combating terrorism,** since terrorist groups that can learn effectively can pose a more potent threat than do organizations that are unable to change and adapt.

An understanding of terrorist group learning can also assist in developing metrics for efforts to combat terrorism by providing an additional approach for assessing the effects of countermeasures on terrorist group capabilities.

About This Study

This study addresses two basic questions:

- What is known about how terrorist groups learn?
- Can such knowledge be used by law enforcement and intelligence personnel in their efforts to combat terrorism?

To answer these questions, we have (1) examined theory and data about how organizations learn, drawn from the organizational behavior and management literature, and (2) developed in-depth case studies of learning in a variety of terrorist groups through literature research and interviews with intelligence and law enforcement professionals who have had direct experience with terrorist groups.[2]

Using analytical frameworks drawn from the organizational-theory literature to assist in framing questions about what organizations must do to learn, we examined terrorist groups that have been successful learners in order to focus on those behaviors of greatest concern. Discussions with intelligence and law enforcement professionals enabled us to explore the applicability and utility of organizational-learning-focused approaches to analysis and operational planning for combating terrorism.

Figure S.1
Component Processes of Organizational Learning

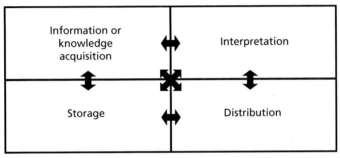

RAND *MG331-S.1*

Terrorist groups present a moving target that can prove very difficult to hit. Effective efforts to combat terrorism require the ability to anticipate how and where groups are evolving over time. Beyond simply describing how such groups change—for example, tracking differences in weapons they use or how well they use them—we need to understand the mechanisms through which those changes occur. Drawing on the organizational-theory literature, we adopted a model of learning as a four-part process, comprising acquiring, interpreting, distributing, and storing information and knowledge (Figure S.1). By breaking down the composite and complex process of "learning" into discrete pieces, this model helps frame specific and actionable questions about how individual terrorist groups learn. Sufficiently detailed information on the four subprocesses in the model could assist law enforcement and intelligence professionals in carrying out the three key functions shown in Figure S.2: *detecting* terrorist groups' efforts to change and adapt, *anticipating* whether those efforts will be successful, and *acting* to limit terrorist groups' ability to learn or undermine their learning efforts.

---

[2] This approach has been applied previously to the analysis of drug cartels and transnational criminal organizations (see Kenney, 2002, 2003b).

Figure S.2
Phases of Law Enforcement and Intelligence Activity to Counter Terrorist Group Efforts to Change and Adapt

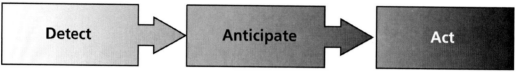

RAND *MG331-S.2*

Detecting Terrorist Groups' Efforts to Change

Although the efforts of terrorist groups to adapt and learn are frequently easy to see in hindsight, they are much more difficult to detect before they are fully realized. Detection is critical, however, if terrorist groups are to be denied the advantage of surprise in their tactics and operations. Intelligence and law enforcement analysts must have access to specific types of information, the ability to extract that information from the noisy background of collected intelligence, and the analytical tools to discern what the information means in terms of terrorist group adaptive activities.

Integrating an understanding of organizational learning into the intelligence collection and analysis process could help ensure that key information about terrorist groups' adaptive efforts is not overlooked. Providing a structure for framing clear, actionable questions about the specific processes of terrorist group learning could increase the possibility that the right information will be collected and will therefore be available to analysts studying particular groups. Similarly, a clear model of how terrorist organizations learn would provide an alternative analytical framework for examining new intelligence. Such a framework would help to ensure that data signaling terrorist group learning activities are not missed in the daily stream of collected intelligence. Having a clear understanding of organizational learning processes would also provide a context for assessing more fully the potential "learning implications" of a terrorist group's current activities. Having such an alternative lens through which to view new information could be critical—for example, individual operations that appear detrimental to a terrorist group's interests from a strategic or organizational perspective may have very different implications when viewed from the perspective of the group's learning goals.

Key Findings: Detecting Terrorist Groups' Efforts to Change

• Use frameworks describing organizational learning by terrorist organizations to focus intelligence collection and ensure that necessary information is collected and terrorists' efforts to change are not overlooked.

• Use a learning-focused analytical framework for assessing collected intelligence to help capture and understand the learning implications of group activities.

Anticipating the Outcomes of Terrorist Groups' Efforts to Change

It is always worrisome when a terrorist group decides to pursue damaging new weapons or to adopt a new tactic. But whether or not such a decision actually increases the threat posed by the group depends on whether the terrorists can bring their plans to fruition. Accurately assessing the implications of a shift in a terrorist group's intent or activities—i.e., determining whether the threat it is trying to pose is credible—requires a judgment about the likelihood of the group succeeding in its plans. Because successful learning dramatically increases a terrorist group's ability to do what it wants to do, understanding how the group learns can help analysts anticipate whether the group will succeed in its efforts. To better understand how a terrorist group learns, the analyst can (1) examine the group and its circumstances to assess how their characteristics will affect its ability to learn and (2) examine what the group is trying to accomplish to assess whether the strategies it has adopted will bring together the ingredients needed to succeed.

Earlier research has identified a range of characteristics associated with a group's ability to learn effectively. Details about the nature of an organization's structure and interconnections, its membership, its environment, and the specific activities it is carrying out can all contribute to judgments about a group's learning potential. Examining the variables that affect a terrorist organization's ability to succeed (Figure S.3)

Figure S.3
Characteristics That Affect Terrorist Group Learning Abilities

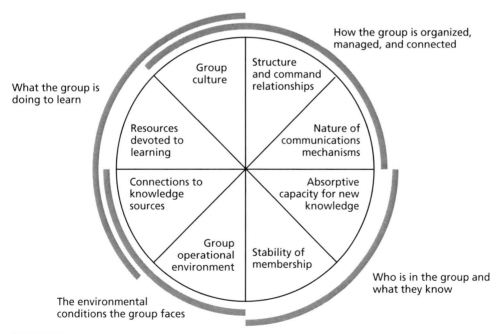

RAND *MG331-S.3*

can enable analysts to better assess the credibility of the threat posed by the organization.

To learn successfully, an organization must combine different types of knowledge. *Explicit* knowledge—e.g., recipes for explosive materials, blueprints for attractive targets, weapons or other technologies—can be transferred readily to a terrorist group, provided it can find an appropriate and willing source. *Tacit* knowledge—e.g., proficiency in mixing explosives safely or the military expertise and operational intuition needed to plan an operation well—is more difficult to transfer from one group to another. To the extent that the analyst can evaluate the combinations of explicit and tacit knowledge needed for an organization's plans, he or she can assess the likelihood the organization's strategy for gathering that knowledge and implementing its plans will be successful.

Key Findings: Anticipating the Outcomes of Terrorist Groups' Efforts to Change

- Gather information about the characteristics of terrorist groups' structures and interconnections, membership, environment, and activities that are specifically relevant to assessing the likely outcome of their attempts to adapt and evolve.
- Examine the varied paths and combinations of knowledge relevant to terrorist groups' learning goals to enable better assessment of the potential success of their efforts to learn.

Acting More Effectively to Thwart Terrorist Efforts

An understanding of how terrorist groups learn can contribute to shaping approaches for combating terrorism. Terrorist groups' learning capabilities define the options they have available to defeat security measures and counter the actions of security forces. Such groups have devoted considerable effort to foiling the information-gathering efforts of intelligence and law enforcement organizations and have informed their attack plans by direct study and observation of security forces' tactics and procedures. If the ways terrorist groups learn to get around countermeasures can be understood and anticipated, the design and application of those countermeasures can be improved. A detailed understanding of group learning processes could make it possible to design countermeasures to directly address or even take advantage of terrorist groups' attempts to learn. Targeted attacks on a group's "learning systems" could degrade the group's ability to adapt over time.[3] Potential strategies include the following:

---

[3] It should be noted, however, that terrorist groups could respond to such efforts by subsequently altering their learning processes.

- Limiting the terrorist group's access to critical knowledge resources
- Identifying and preventing acquisition of novel technologies and weapons
- Locating and targeting a terrorist group's "learning leadership"—those individuals critical to the ability to carry out organizational learning processes
- Identifying and breaking critical connections among terrorist group members
- Designing strategies for combating terrorism to maximize the "learning burden" placed on terrorist groups and limit their chances of adapting to get around it
- Denying terrorist groups the safe haven needed for experimentation and innovation

Beyond simply seeking to prevent a terrorist group from learning, strategies for combating terrorism could be designed to shape group learning in more subtle ways. With sufficient information on terrorist groups' learning processes, intelligence and law enforcement organizations could potentially affect the nature and outcome of group learning activities. Strategies utilizing deception, misinformation, and other psychological techniques could be applied to steer terrorist group learning in specific directions or influence the apparent results of their efforts. Such indirect approaches would require significant knowledge about a terrorist group's learning efforts and even then would never be guaranteed success, but they could serve as useful alternative or complementary tactics.

Key Findings: Acting More Effectively to Thwart Terrorist Efforts

- Use an understanding of terrorist groups' learning capabilities to improve planning for combating terrorism. Shape countermeasures to resist efforts to circumvent or defeat them.
- Apply models of terrorist groups' learning behaviors to the design of novel countermeasures that specifically target their ability to adapt and change.
- Seek out opportunities to use terrorist groups' learning activities against them by guiding their efforts or shaping the outcomes of those efforts to reduce the groups' capabilities and potential threat levels.

Conclusions

Although no single method or analytical approach will be applicable to all terrorist groups in all circumstances, an understanding of how groups learn would be a valuable addition to the intelligence and law enforcement "tool box" for analysis and operational planning of efforts to combat terrorism. However, to gain such an understanding, sufficient information about a terrorist group's learning behavior must be collected and available. Without the information needed to discern how a terrorist group is structured, to describe its learning processes, and to determine how its learning efforts should be assessed, these approaches will provide little benefit to the analyst. In some cases, such information may be collected in the course of general intelligence gathering on a terrorist group; in other cases, specific efforts may be required. Even for the groups examined in this study—terrorist organizations that have been the focus of significant analytical attention over many years—information on the learning process is not always easy to find. Studies of groups carried out for other reasons have sometimes provided insights about learning, but even then, blind spots remain, particularly regarding the internal components of the process, such as interpretation and decisionmaking activities, which are perhaps of greatest interest to the analyst studying learning behavior.

When the necessary information is available, however, analytical frameworks describing organizational learning can be of great value. By providing a fuller picture of how terrorist groups try to adapt and evolve over time, such frameworks can help in understanding the behavior of individual groups and the level of threat they pose; developing effective counterstrategies to detect and thwart their efforts; and appropriately allocating resources among potential and proven adversaries in the context of a multipronged approach to combating terrorism.

Acknowledgments

The members of the research team would like to extend their thanks to the many individuals in governments, academic institutions, and other organizations around the world who gave generously of their time and expertise as the study progressed. Study workshop participants from a variety of law enforcement, homeland security, and intelligence agencies provided critical input that made the analysis possible. Because of the sensitivity of the topics involved, these outside contributors are not identified here, but the necessity of maintaining their anonymity in no way diminishes our gratitude for their participation.

We gratefully acknowledge the funding from the National Institute of Justice that supported this research. The direct assistance and support we received from Marvene O'Rourke and Sandra Woerle, who served as the NIJ grant monitors for this effort through the period of research and writing, were also invaluable in facilitating our efforts.

We also gratefully acknowledge the contributions of our reviewers, Dennis Pluchinsky and Terrence Kelly. The report benefited greatly from their thoughtful and thorough reviews and the insights and suggestions they provided.

A number of our RAND colleagues gave generously of their time and insights. We would like to acknowledge Claude Berrebi, Sara Daly, Bruce Don, David Frelinger, Scott Gerwehr, Bruce Hoffman, Angel Rabasa, Bill Rosenau, and Mike Wermuth. Susan Bohandy of RAND's Research Communications Group provided valuable assistance and input that greatly improved the report. Jeremy Roth and Merril Micelli provided administrative support for both the project workshop and the overall project. Janet DeLand also provided extremely valuable input during the final edit of the text that greatly improved the readability of the report.

Finally, we would like to acknowledge Patricia Touw, Anduin Touw, Craig DeAlmeida, and Katherine DeAlmeida, who provided research and editing assistance during various phases of the study.

Abbreviations and Acronyms

Aum	Aum Shinrikyo
ELF/ALF	Earth Liberation Front/Animal Liberation Front
ETA	Basque Fatherland and Liberty
FARC	Revolutionary Armed Forces of Colombia
JI	Jemaah Islamiyah
LTTE	Liberation Tigers of Tamil Eelam
PIRA	Provisional Irish Republican Army
PLO	Palestinian Liberation Organization
RPG	rocket-propelled grenade
TOW	tube-launched, optically tracked, wire-guided (missile)

CHAPTER ONE

Introduction

Early in its campaign in Northern Ireland, the Provisional Irish Republican Army (PIRA) faced a problem. Improving security forces' activities and the strengthening of military bases and police stations made it increasingly difficult for the Provisionals to stage attacks on these targets with their preferred weapons. To solve this problem, PIRA made the decision to pursue a new weapon—the mortar.

Although PIRA could have sought out mortars from the international arms market, the group chose to build its own. Reportedly drawing on knowledge from military reference books, the Provisionals began to manufacture mortar units in local machine shops and safe houses. PIRA's path to developing mortar technology was not a smooth one. Early versions of the weapons threw their shells far off course, sometimes exploding in residential areas and schools, killing and maiming civilians. Shells that reached their targets often didn't explode or exploded ineffectively. Units with design defects exploded in the mortar tube, killing the PIRA members attempting to use them.

PIRA made many modifications to their mortars' designs to correct their flaws and better adapt them to the group's operational needs. The Provisionals' engineers observed the performance of their creations, identified their shortcomings, experimented with alternative designs, and introduced the new models into the group's arsenal. Cells within PIRA became expert in the use of the weapon and applied their expertise both to constructing new mortar designs and to applying the weapons in high-profile attack operations. The group was innovative in its tactics. It built mortars into vehicles for greater mobility and fitted them with timers so individual Provisionals could place the weapons and disappear long before an attack took place.

Over time, the group's learning and engineering efforts paid off, and knowledge of how to make and use mortars effectively was distributed among its members, becoming a core part of the organization's capabilities. The group's perseverance reaped terrible dividends late in its operational career, as mortars made it possible to stage some of PIRA's highest-profile operations: a direct attack on the British Prime Minister's residence at 10 Downing Street, multiple mortar attacks on

Heathrow Airport, and an attack on the police station at Newry which claimed the lives of nine members of the Royal Ulster Constabulary.[1]

Terrorism[2] and insurgent violence have become constant threats in today's world. Nearly every day, nonstate groups in different countries carry out violent actions, many of which can be characterized as terrorism. The threat of such violence drives ongoing global military action, and the need to protect the U.S. homeland against terrorist attack is a primary shaper of the country's domestic political agenda.[3]

The experience of PIRA described above illustrates the importance of terrorist groups' ability to change and adapt. Faced with a challenge to their operational capability, PIRA shifted, adopting a new attack form that reconstituted the threat they could pose. The ability to modify tactics and behaviors is critical across all areas of terrorist group operations.[4] Such adaptive behaviors can enable terrorist groups to

- Become more effective at applying their chosen tactics and weapons[5]
- Adopt new, often increasingly damaging tactics and weapons
- Alter their behavior in an effort to fend off attempts to infiltrate, undermine, and destroy them[6]

The ability of terrorist organizations to change their operations effectively over time is inherently linked to their ability to learn.[7] While changes in society, coun-

---

[1] Narrative adapted from Bell, 1998b; Geraghty, 2000; Glover, 1978; Harnden, 2000; O'Callaghan, 1999; Urban, 1992.

[2] In this report, we adopt the convention that *terrorism* is a tactic—the systematic and premeditated use, or threatened use, of violence by nonstate groups to further political or social objectives to coerce an audience larger than those directly affected. With terrorism defined as a tactic, it follows that individual organizations are not inherently "terrorist." We use the terms "terrorist group" and "terrorist organization" as shorthand for "group that has chosen to utilize terrorism."

[3] Though many of the violent substate groups discussed in this study use tactics that are not purely terroristic in nature—for example, mixing traditional military operations against opposing security forces with terrorist bombings or assassinations—we use "terrorism," "terrorist violence," and "counterterrorism" as generic descriptors of groups' violent activities and government efforts to counter them.

[4] For a variety of discussions of change and adaptation in terrorism and terrorist group activities, see Cragin and Daly, 2004; Crenshaw, 2001; Gerwehr and Glenn, 2003, pp. 49–53; Hoffman, 2001; Jackson, 2001; Kitfield, 2001; Stern, 2003; Thomas and Casebeer, 2004, pp. 35–38. We particularly acknowledge Lutes (2001), an unpublished paper that did not come to our attention until late in the study. Lutes brings the literature on organizational learning to bear on terrorism, specifically on al Qaeda.

[5] Training of group members is a primary route through which organizations carry out this organizational learning function.

[6] This adaptation can include the adoption of new learning behaviors.

[7] While change in the way a group carries out its activities is frequently indicative of learning, the occurrence of change is not sufficient to indicate that organizational learning has occurred. Changes are not necessarily intentional; they can be made unintentionally or for exogenous reasons incidental to the behavior that is changed (e.g., a change may occur in one area simply as a result of a change made in another). In this study, we define learning

termeasures, or shifts in the public's reactions to types of attacks might provide the *motivation* for change, a terrorist group cannot adapt automatically. New tactics and novel capabilities do not become available without effort. Terrorist groups do not improve their ability to execute operations or increase their level of expertise with weapons simply because they want to do so. Organizations must be able to learn in order to identify opportunities and to have the wherewithal to take advantage of them with significant chances of success. The ability to learn marks the difference between a lucky organization that may fortuitously discover the solutions to its problems and a consistently effective one that can systematically act to fulfill its needs and advance its goals in a dynamic environment.

Terrorist groups' learning capabilities pose a significant challenge to the ability of law enforcement and intelligence organizations to protect the public. In addressing the threat posed by terrorism, such organizations face three central challenges:

- **Assessing threats and understanding terrorist group behavior.** Understanding a terrorist group's intentions and capabilities, the types of operations it may attempt, and its chances of being successful when it stages an operation is critical for effective efforts to combat terrorism. Because terrorist organizations are moving targets, the analyst must understand them in a dynamic context—not just what the organization is today, but what it might be tomorrow. Law enforcement and intelligence organizations must also rapidly identify the groups or individuals responsible for terrorist incidents so that action can be taken in response.
- **Developing and implementing counterstrategies.** Proactively defeating terrorism requires the ability to discover terrorist group activities, gather needed evidence and intelligence information, and disrupt operations and destroy group infrastructures and capabilities. To develop effective strategies for combating terrorism, law enforcement and intelligence action must be shaped so that it is appropriate for the specific situations of particular groups and the environments in which they operate.
- **Allocating resources and developing metrics to assess success in combating terrorism.** Because the resources that can be devoted to combating terrorism are finite, decisions must be made about how and where those resources should be allocated. Knowledge of terrorist groups' intent helps to make those decisions. There is less pressure to devote resources to thwarting the efforts of groups that are not interested in attacking a nation or its interests. However, the remaining

---

as sustained changes that involve intentional action by or within a group at some point—such as one or more of the following: intentional seeking of new knowledge or new ways of doing things; intentional evaluation of behaviors, new or old, that leads to efforts to retain valuable behaviors and discard others; and/or intentional dissemination of knowledge within a group or among groups when such knowledge is deemed useful or beneficial. Furthermore, we categorize as learning only changes that are beneficial to the terrorist group.

groups frequently pose more potential threats than it is possible to target with the resources available. Decisions must be made about deploying resources, and metrics must be developed to measure the results of those decisions to ensure that the most serious threats to national security and human life are being addressed.[8]

An understanding of how terrorist organizations learn may allow analysts to get inside a group's efforts to change and adapt and could thereby help the law enforcement and intelligence communities address all three challenges. Insights about terrorist group learning processes provide an approach to building an understanding of the dynamics of terrorist organizations, not just by tracking data on how they change but by exploring the ways those changes are realized. Such an understanding could facilitate better threat assessment and could also play a part in assigning responsibility for past terrorist incidents. Organizations' "learning histories" can help identify what group or groups could plausibly have carried out specific attacks.

In addition, an understanding of group learning processes might also help analysts identify and exploit key weaknesses in a group's organizational and operational makeup. Measures of terrorist group learning can help to separate groups whose capabilities may be bounded by an inability to adapt from those that can more readily shift to pose greater levels of threat, providing a key input to threat assessment and resource allocation.

About This Study

This research effort addresses two basic questions:

- What is known about how terrorist groups learn?
- Can that knowledge be used by law enforcement and intelligence personnel in their efforts to combat terrorism?

To answer these questions, we designed a methodology to explore why and what terrorist groups learn, to gain insights into their learning processes, and to identify ways in which the law enforcement and intelligence communities might apply those insights. The research process comprised four main tasks:

1. **Review of the literature on organizational learning.** The rich literature on learning in organizations is focused predominantly on learning in legitimate

---

[8] See Cragin and Daly, 2004, for a discussion of the relative threat posed by terrorist organizations as a function of their differing capabilities and intentions.

groups, particularly commercial organizations, but it provides a wealth of models and hypotheses on group learning practices that can be applied to terrorist groups. Later phases of our study were informed by ideas and concepts drawn from this literature.

2. **Review of available literature on terrorism and insurgent violence.** We reviewed the published literature and other data sources on groups that have used terrorism to assess what was already known about organizational learning activities in such groups and to assist in selecting individual groups for detailed study.

3. **Terrorist group case studies.** The research process consisted primarily of preparing and reviewing a set of case studies of organizations that have used terrorism as a component of their violent activities. We selected five organizations for these case studies:[9]

- Aum Shinrikyo
- Hizballah
- Jemaah Islamiyah (JI)
- Provisional Irish Republican Army (PIRA)
- The Radical Environmentalist Movement

These groups, having a variety of characteristics, were selected to cover the full spectrum of organizations that have used terrorism: Aum Shinrikyo is a religious cult that pursued chemical and biological weapons; Hizballah is a social and political movement with insurgent and terrorist aims and activities; JI is a smaller, better defined terrorist group linked to and influenced by the global *jihadist* movement; PIRA is a traditional ethnic terrorist group with a long operational history; and the radical environmentalist movement (focusing on terrorist activities claimed by organizations identified as the Earth Liberation Front and the Animal Liberation Front, among others)[10] is an example of a much less-defined

---

[9] Al Qaeda was deliberately *not* selected to be a case study group. The goal of the study was to examine organizational learning across different types of terrorist organizations to find commonalities and differences among their experiences. The rapid change occurring in al Qaeda during the study period and the volume of information available made it such a complex subject that we would not have been able to satisfactorily examine a sufficient number of other terrorist groups.

[10] It should be noted that the radical environmental movement is significantly different from the other groups examined in this study. Examining the actions claimed by organizations identifying themselves as the Earth Liberation Front (ELF), the Animal Liberation Front (ALF), and others from the perspective that they are carried out by a defined "group" is problematic as these organizations function as pieces within a broader ideological movement, rather than defined and bounded groups in a traditional sense. However, because of assumed cross-membership of individuals and cross-fertilization among many groups within the radical environmentalist movement, law enforcement and counterterrorism efforts frequently treat ELF, ALF, and affiliated groups as a single organization for analytical purposes, while recognizing that the organization's diversity adds a unique dynamic to such analyses. In this study we will refer to these groups as either radical environmentalists or, for shorthand purposes, ELF/ALF. Given the relevance of similar movements in modern terrorism—e.g., extremist right-wing, anti-globalization, violent anti-abortion, and global *jihad* movements—the differences between the learning processes of ELF/ALF and those of more traditional organizations are of significant interest.

terrorist "front" of a broader ideological movement. These organizations are described in more detail in the Appendix to this report.

In addition, to focus the study on learning behavior, we chose terrorist groups that have a reputation for innovative activities.[11] The wide variety of group types selected was intentional—addressing the study's research questions required examining the relevance and utility of organizational learning theories and frameworks across a range of terrorist groups.

To provide a common approach and structure for the individual case studies, the researcher examining each terrorist group began his or her work with a common set of areas to explore, including the group's motivations for learning, the areas it chose to learn, the outcomes, and—to the extent possible—how it carried out its learning efforts. The case study process included review of available published information on each group's learning activities, supplemented by examination of other information sources and interviews with experts in the academic, intelligence, and law enforcement communities who had direct experience with the groups being studied.

4. **Project workshop.** We invited practitioners from law enforcement and the intelligence community, along with academic experts, to participate in a workshop held concurrently in RAND's Washington, DC, and Santa Monica, CA, offices on September 29, 2004. Approximately 25 individuals participated in the workshop, where discussions were held on a not-for-attribution basis. The workshop focused

---

[11] Throughout this report, terrorist groups that can learn effectively are contrasted with groups that are not effective learners and, as a result, pose less serious levels of threat. Because of the design of the study, specific groups that learn poorly were not examined in detail and are generally cited as a class rather than as individual groups. Terrorism-incident databases and compendia, such as the Memorial Institute for the Prevention of Terrorism's *Terrorism Knowledge Base* (http://www.tkb.org), provide a range of examples of groups that are poor learners— groups that staged only single types of attacks of limited effectiveness, communicated so poorly that their agenda and intent was difficult to discern, or were rapidly rolled up by security and law enforcement. It should be noted that even terrorist groups that one might consider poor learners overall obviously learned in some areas, but their inability to do so in the areas most critical to their effectiveness limited their impact. Such groups include the following:

- The Tupac Katari Guerrilla Army in Bolivia was active for two years. It had approximately 100 members but did not learn what was needed to maintain its activities after its leadership was captured (http://www.tkb.org/ Group.jsp?groupID=4289).
- Terra Lliure in Spain disbanded after approximately 20 years, during which it never developed effective strategies to build significant support among the Catalan population it sought to champion (http://www.tkb.org/ Group.jsp?groupID=4281).
- The Free Papua Movement, partially due to its goals and ideology, did not pursue technologies that would pose a significant threat (http://www.tkb.org/Group.jsp?groupID=4023).
- Black Star in Greece, which carried out attacks via two tactics—using gas canister bombs and setting cars on fire—demonstrated neither the interest nor the ability to carry out operational learning in its attack modes (http://www.tkb.org/Group.jsp?groupID=32).

A number of other terrorist groups carried out only one or a handful of attacks before disbanding, disappearing, or being arrested without any of their stated goals accomplished. Assessing such groups is difficult, however, as the "new" terrorist groups could be established organizations adopting a cover name for a few operations.

on practical insights into how to improve the design of policies for combating terrorism. Starting with the preliminary results of the case studies, the discussion explored how analytical approaches based on organizational learning might be relevant and applicable to combating terrorism.

About This Report

This report synthesizes the results of the study, combining input from the organizational learning literature, published literature on terrorist and insurgent groups, and insights drawn from the case studies and workshop discussions. Chapter Two describes organizational learning. Chapter Three examines terrorist groups' need to learn in order to change effectively. Chapter Four assesses the utility of understanding terrorist group learning in planning and implementing efforts to combat terrorism and, therefore, contains the core observations that may be most useful to law enforcement and intelligence agencies as they craft programs and operations for combating terrorism. The report does not present explicit recommendations; rather, it outlines a framework that should be useful both for current implementation and for identifying areas requiring further study. Chapter Five addresses the limits of analytical approaches based on organizational learning, and the study's conclusions are summarized in Chapter Six.

Although this report uses selected examples and illustrations from the case studies to support its discussion of applying an understanding of organizational learning to combating terrorism, it does not capture the full richness of detail included in the individual cases. The case studies are described in detail in a companion volume, *Aptitude for Destruction, Volume 2: Case Studies of Organizational Learning in Five Terrorist Groups*, MG-332-NIJ, 2005.

CHAPTER TWO

What Is Organizational Learning?

Organizational learning is a process through which a group acquires new knowledge or technology that it then uses to make better strategic decisions, improve its ability to develop and apply specific tactics, and increase its chance of success in its operations.[1] In short, learning is change aimed at improving a group's performance; we would not call change that is detrimental *learning*.[2]

While individual members of a group must build new skills and knowledge in order for organizational learning to take place, learning at the organizational level is more than simply the sum of what each individual member knows or can do. An organization is a system that structures, stores, and influences what and how its members learn (Fiol and Lyles, 1985; Hedberg, 1981; Shrivastava, 1983). As such, it possesses a "memory" greater than that of any individual member: "Members [of an organization] come and go, and leadership changes, but organizations' memories preserve certain behaviors, mental maps, norms and values over time" (Easterby-Smith et al., 2000). This "organizational memory" enables an organization to utilize the capabilities of individual members to achieve group goals while reducing its dependence on any one person. When knowledge is *organizational*, a group has captured new or expanded capabilities in such a way that it does not depend on particular individuals to exploit them.

Although they are significantly different from the private-sector companies that are the focus of much of the literature on organizational learning, terrorist groups *are* organizations. To be successful, they must change; and to change effectively, they must learn. Operating in extremely volatile environments, they must capture their learning at an organizational level in order to survive. By doing so, they gain critical advantages: They can gather the information they need more readily than any single individual could; they can interpret that information through the diverse lenses of

---

[1] The literature on organizational learning offers a range of definitions that differ with regard to, for example, what a group must demonstrate to show learning, whether the process must be intentional, and whether the knowledge gained must be relevant to an organization's actions and goals. Our definition is roughly equivalent to that of Miller (1996).

[2] However, organizational processes that enable learning can teach destructive behavior if they are misinformed.

many different members; they can transmit information from an original learner to other group members, thereby reducing the risk of losing important knowledge if any one member is lost.[3] The following sections describe the process of organizational learning in terrorist groups, drawing on illustrations from the description of PIRA's acquisition of mortar technologies presented in Chapter One.

Organizational Learning as a Four-Part Process

Learning can be characterized as a process comprising four component subprocesses: acquiring, interpreting, distributing, and storing information and knowledge.[4,5] Figure 2.1 shows a model of this process. All four subprocesses must be carried out successfully for knowledge to become organizational—that is, clearly tied to group objectives, accessible to many different group members, and resistant to the loss of individual members. The subprocesses are interrelated and can occur in different orders, depending on context. For example, when the individuals who acquire new information or knowledge are also qualified to interpret it, there is no need to distribute it to anyone else in the group before it can be utilized. But when the members with the expertise to make use of new information are not the ones who collected it, the information first needs to be transferred. PIRA's mortar development is a case in point. The members who used mortars to stage attacks could assess their

Figure 2.1
Component Processes of Organizational Learning

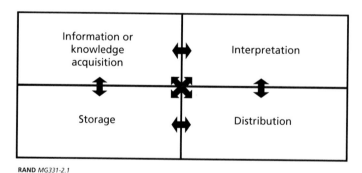

RAND MG331-2.1

---

[3] Argyris and Schön (1978) best summarize the advantages and limitations of organizational learning.

[4] Lutes (2001) presents a similar four-stage model, also applied to terrorist organizations.

[5] Romme and Dillen (1997) present a brief but detailed treatment of organizational learning as an information process. This model also draws on Barnett's (n.d.) description of organizational learning (cited in Lipshitz et al., 2002), which defines it as "an experience-based process through which knowledge about action-outcome relationships develops, is encoded in routines, is embedded in organizational memory and changes collective behavior."

operations, make judgments about their use of the devices, and apply tactical improvements to the way they used them. They had no immediate need to distribute this information to other members of the group. But new technical information on the ways mortars were failing probably had to be transferred to the group's engineers, who could understand its implications and apply it to improve the next generation of weapons.

Acquisition

In order to learn, groups must acquire the information or knowledge[6] they need to assess the value of their current activities, understand their effects, and identify changes they need to make to their future behavior to improve performance. They can both reach to external sources for information and mine the knowledge of their own members.

Acquiring Information or Knowledge from External Sources

Organizations of all sizes obtain information and knowledge from external sources, but small organizations are much more likely to need to look outside frequently, because they can seldom find all of the knowledge they need within the group. Some common external resources are described below.

Vicarious Experience. Observing the activities of other groups to glean insights is the least demanding way of gathering information, since it usually requires little effort on the part of the observing group. Vicarious experience usually provides only incomplete insights, however, because observers can watch only the effects of an operation and may not gain all the information or knowledge they would need to duplicate it.

Cooperation with Other Organizations. Groups can access information or knowledge from other groups engaged in similar activities (Romme and Dillen, 1997). Different organizations can form a variety of joint efforts and interactions aimed at specific goals. When the aims and culture of other organizations are compatible with those of the group seeking information or knowledge, such organizations can be a very valuable resource. They may be less useful when their goals or culture diverge, because these differences can impede the flow of information or knowledge between the groups (Jones, 1991).

---

[6] The difference between information and knowledge is mainly the degree of relevance and adaptation to the needs and applications of an organization. Information could be any new data that may or may not be useful and may need considerable other information, expertise, etc., in order to be gainfully applied. Knowledge is more "finished"—it is already partially adapted to the needs of a group or comes with more of the ingredients needed for use. In the context of the discussion in this report, some sources of information are likely to provide information rather than knowledge, but drawing a rigorous distinction between the two is not critical. In general, we will use *knowledge* as an inclusive term that can capture both.

Outside Human Resources. If a group can locate the right individual experts, it can draw on their expertise either by recruiting them into the organization or by engaging them as consultants.

Outside Knowledge Sources or Technologies. Acquiring potentially useful technologies or other knowledge sources—ranging from weapons to blueprints of desirable targets—can rapidly increase a group's capabilities. PIRA's acquisition of plans to manufacture mortars is an example of a group using an external knowledge source. For certain types of knowledge, public and electronic sources, such as the Internet, can be highly useful. However, acquiring knowledge, whether it is a technology or some other source of relevant data, generally does not mean that one has all the related information required to use that knowledge effectively. Therefore, groups may need to draw on other sources to gain the additional required information.

Acquiring Information or Knowledge from Internal Sources

Groups commonly gather or develop new information or knowledge within their ranks. They draw on three main sources: congenital knowledge, direct experience, and internal knowledge development.

Congenital Knowledge. The information that an organization inherits from its founding leaders and members is very important early in its development. As the environment changes and the group matures, other sources of knowledge become more important.

Direct Experience ("Learning by Doing"). A group's ongoing activities provide valuable information and spur knowledge development. Groups frequently draw on this knowledge source unintentionally and unsystematically as they recognize mistakes that offer lessons on how to improve over time (Cyert and March, 1963). Deliberate efforts to garner information in this way usually take the form of some sort of evaluation, such as an after-action review or lessons-learned process. PIRA's improvements in their use of mortars drew on information gained in their initial failures; the group was learning by doing.

Internal Development of Knowledge. A group may be able to develop new knowledge internally. Internal research and development efforts can be aimed at such things as crafting new tactics and weapons to support group operations. The development of mortars by PIRA's own engineering department is an example of such activity. Information and knowledge can also be developed through training, where a group can experiment with and test new concepts and technologies.

Interpretation

Without the ability to assess the meaning and value of information or new knowledge it acquires, a group cannot put that information or knowledge to use (Huber,

1991). The group must learn lessons and make judgments about three classes of activities:[7]

- **Current activities.** Are the group's actions effective? Are they moving the group toward its overall strategic goals? How can the group alter these actions to make them more successful?
- **Possible future activities.** Would a new tactic or technology help the group?[8] Does the group know what it needs to know to use that tactic or technology? Is the group likely to be able to use it successfully?
- **Older or invalidated knowledge and procedures.** Is older knowledge still useful? Are established routines still effective? Should they be discarded in order to adopt newer operating procedures (Hedberg, 1981; McGill and Slocum, Jr., 1993)?

For interpretation to be most effective, the group must have both the knowledge needed to make sense of new information and the time and opportunity to think through what it means. Being able to interpret information within a useful time interval is also critical, and culture is key: The group must be open-minded enough to recognize when its circumstances have changed or a particular approach is not working, rather than adhering inflexibly to previous assumptions.

Distribution

Distribution plays a critical role in advancing the learning process. Organizational learning requires that knowledge get to the right people in the group. The more broadly information is distributed within an organization, the more likely it is to be interpreted and to be interpreted in multiple ways, which increases the likelihood that the group will be able to utilize it effectively. Distribution also plays a central role in facilitating the storage of information and increasing its availability for later use. Effective distribution significantly lowers the risk that an organization's learning will deteriorate (Huber, 1991). However, for terrorist organizations, this may come at the price of increased vulnerability to compromise and penetration because of the

---

[7] Much of the following discussion is framed in a language consistent with viewing terrorist groups and decisionmakers as essentially rational actors—interpreting information based on some concept of the organization's goals and making decisions on the basis of whether an activity does or does not contribute to them. Other elements of the literature on terrorist group decisionmaking (reviewed recently in McCormick, 2003) provide different "frames" through which to view the interpretation activities of terrorist groups. The analyses reported here do not depend on the specific decisionmaking model appropriate for a given terrorist organization; a group can learn, no matter what interpretive model it applies, and can make rational decisions and choices within its interpretive frame, though the specifics of its model would be a primary shaper of the aims of its learning efforts.

[8] Dolnik and Bhattacharjee (2002) describe such a notional interpretation process regarding Hamas's choice to pursue and use different types of weapons.

possibility of interception of communications traffic by law enforcement or intelligence organizations.

Storage

Groups must retain information and knowledge to ensure that they can access them in the future. Newer organizations usually keep knowledge almost exclusively in the individual memories of group members. In PIRA, individuals were a key repository of the group's expertise in mortar use. However, individual memories are highly vulnerable places in which to preserve knowledge (Carley, 1992; Kim, 1993), so established groups tend to favor other repositories:

- **Language, rituals, and symbols.** Storing knowledge in these mechanisms helps to standardize it. Language, rituals, and symbols are also very effective for transferring lessons to new group members.
- **Organizational structures.** Because group structures define the activities of all members of the organization, they can provide a durable way to institutionalize some types of organizational lessons.
- **Written and unwritten operating guidelines.** Manuals, recipes, and other types of records codify a group's processes and can be easily passed among group members.
- **External repositories.** Storing information outside a group, e.g., on the Internet or with members of allied organizations, can provide an alternate strategy to ensure the preservation of key knowledge.

The Need to Combine Explicit and Tacit Knowledge

When PIRA set out to acquire mortars, it had to gain knowledge of various types before its efforts could be successful. To fabricate the weapons, the group needed plans, which it reportedly obtained from military reference books. Such books are examples of *explicit knowledge*, knowledge that is preserved in a physical form—in documents describing activities, blueprints or instructions, and technological systems or devices. This type of knowledge can be transferred from one individual or group to another relatively easily; doing so may entail no more than handing someone a book or downloading a photograph.[9] PIRA could also have chosen to acquire mortars on the international arms market, in which case the weapons themselves would have constituted the majority of the explicit knowledge PIRA needed to attain the capability.

---

[9] Different groups attempting a task described in an explicit format will perform that task similarly, because the knowledge is transferred uniformly (Edmonson et al., 2003).

To use mortars effectively, however, PIRA needed more than just the weapons themselves. It also needed to develop the expertise needed to manufacture the weapons so that they would function properly and the expertise to use them well. The knowledge required to gain expertise is largely *tacit knowledge*—more-abstract knowledge held by individuals. The most common example is the knowledge and skill, often intuitive, that an expert builds over the course of his or her career. Because this type of knowledge is hard to articulate, much less codify,[10] it is much more difficult to transfer than explicit knowledge. The individual seeking the knowledge often has to meet the expert face to face. The development of the right tacit knowledge within PIRA eventually meant that the group could use mortars with consistent effectiveness.

The PIRA story is not an exception; few activities require either explicit or tacit knowledge alone. Acquiring new information, knowledge, or technology from an explicit source is usually only a group's first step. The group must then develop enough tacit knowledge within its ranks to be able to apply the information effectively (Jones, 1991).

Different Forms of Organizational Learning

Different groups need to learn in different ways at different times. This has everything to do with the environment in which a group operates. When conditions are relatively stable, a group may need only to make small changes to the activities it already carries out or the strategies it designs in order to prosper. Once it had acquired mortar technologies, PIRA learned to correct the flaws in its initial designs and improve its ability to use the weapons. Because such *"continuous improvement efforts"* focus on activities a group already performs, they do not challenge existing boundaries, rules, and norms. The change that results can be either unintentional or intentional.

But if the environment shifts considerably, a group needs to make more dramatic changes in order to survive (Wang and Ahmed, 2003). In this case, a group may have to pursue *"discontinuous change"*—learning aimed at entirely new activities or making large shifts in the way the group plans and acts. PIRA's initial acquisition of mortar technologies could be viewed as such a discontinuous change. Depending on the scale of the change, this type of learning can go far beyond the tactical level and may require a group to reevaluate its fundamental strategies, norms, values, structures, processes, and goals. Because it aims at a radical departure from what the

---

[10] This is not to say that it cannot be articulated and codified, thereby being converted to explicit knowledge. That, however, may require a significant investment of resources.

group is already doing, discontinuous change is usually pursued intentionally and requires a more complex learning process than continuous improvement efforts do.

Whether change is continuous or discontinuous is a question of the degree of change involved, not of how fast the change occurs. As a general rule, discontinuous learning tends to happen very quickly, while continuous improvement occurs gradually over a long period of time. But sometimes small-scale changes in a group's environment can happen fast and frequently. The group must be able to respond rapidly to relatively minor changes through appropriate learning efforts in order to survive.

CHAPTER THREE

The Need to Learn in Order to Change Effectively

The effectiveness of a terrorist group that lacks the ability to learn will be determined largely by chance—the chance that its members already have all the necessary skills, the chance that its current tactics are effective against desirable targets and against current countermeasures, and the chance that any accidental or arbitrary shifts the group makes will prove to be beneficial. Since a terrorist group's learning capability is a key determinant of the level of threat it poses, knowledge of that capability is critical for law enforcement and intelligence planners in allocating resources for combating the most dangerous terrorist groups.

A terrorist group that can learn successfully can shape its activities systematically to effectively pursue its organizational goals. Analogous to the three classes of group interpretation activities discussed in Chapter Two, terrorist group activities must be assessed in three time frames:

- **Past behavior.** A learning organization is equipped to assess its tactics and strategic choices, make judgments about what has worked and what has not, and determine whether or not specific actions contributed to achieving its goals.
- **Current activities.** A terrorist group that learns effectively is better prepared to improve its skills and can make better choices in operational planning and execution.
- **Future actions.** A learning organization is prepared to search for and pursue new opportunities and to assess how its strategy and tactics must change if it is to remain effective and survive the pressures of its environment.

A terrorist group's ability to learn at the organizational level can make it both more effective and better able to survive in hostile environments. If a group is able to learn successfully, it can

- Develop, improve, and employ new weapons or tactics to change its capabilities over time

- Improve its members' skills so that they can better apply its current weapons or tactics
- Collect and utilize the intelligence information needed to mount operations effectively
- Thwart countermeasures and improve its chance to survive efforts to destroy it
- Preserve the capabilities it has developed even if individual group members are lost

The operational histories of many terrorist groups, described in our case studies and in the broader terrorism literature, provide examples of the organizational learning processes terrorist organizations have used in each of these five areas, the prices they can pay for not doing so, and the potential benefits of effective learning efforts.

Development, Improvement, and Employment of New Weapons or Tactics

"The more tactics a group has in its repertoire, . . . the greater its flexibility and operational freedom."

A terrorist group has much to gain by building or acquiring new operational capabilities and tactics. The more tactics a group has in its repertoire—from bombings to firearms attacks to kidnappings to unconventional weapons—the greater its flexibility and operational freedom.[1] Having a diverse range of options prepares a terrorist group to deal with complex situations and helps it increase the impact of its operations (Bell, 1998a, p. 183) by

- Addressing shifts in its environment
- Matching tactics precisely to operational needs
- Capitalizing on new opportunities

Addressing Environmental Shifts

Shifts in terrorist groups' environments can gradually devalue their repertoire of attack options—potentially to the point where they become ineffectual. Changes ranging from improved security and hardening of targets to shifts in the public's reaction to different types of attacks can significantly undermine a terrorist group's capabilities. Groups that are effective learners have the opportunity to address such

---

[1] For example, officials interviewed during the study estimated that over the course of its operational career, PIRA developed the ability to use more than 30 different kinds of weapons, including mortars, rocket-propelled grenades (RPGs), explosive devices, and firearms (Jackson, 2005), which it integrated into an even broader range of tactical applications.

changes, modifying and diversifying the ways they stage operations and the technologies they use to do so. The ability to unlearn—to rapidly discard previous modes of operation when they prove ineffective—is similarly essential. For example, when elements of the radical environmental movement realized that their operations in wilderness areas were becoming less effective for advancing their agenda, they shifted their focus from operations such as tree spiking to attacking suburban housing developments (Schwarzen, 2004). This enabled the movement to stage operations that attracted more public attention and also increased its visibility. Aum Shinrikyo and Hizballah also developed new types of weapons and tactics in response to environmental change, sometimes by drawing on expert consultants and other sources of outside knowledge. Aum's learning was driven by the perception that its environment required it to acquire unconventional weapons to defend itself and to advance its apocalyptic agenda (Kaplan and Marshall, 1996). Because of perceived changes in its operational environment, Hizballah shifted its operations from predominantly terrorist attacks on international targets in Beirut toward more direct confrontation with Israeli forces in southern Lebanon (Ranstorp, 1997). Hizballah's organizational learning capabilities enabled it to build the guerrilla-warfare capabilities needed for success in this second phase of its conflict.

Matching Tactics to Operational Needs

All of the case study groups acquired not only the ability to use new weapons, but also the ability to manufacture them. In some groups, manufacturing was quite limited (or confined to single munitions types); for example, ELF/ALF "members" manufactured only incendiary devices, and JI produced only bombs. Other groups, such as PIRA and Hizballah, developed full-scale capabilities to manufacture arms. Learning to manufacture weapons provides a terrorist organization with a more stable and predictable source of arms, as well as the ability to customize weapons over time so that their capabilities better match their operational needs. To adapt to shifts in Israeli forces' tactics, Hizballah produced homemade claymore-type antipersonnel mines that provided significant advantages in targeting security patrols (Cragin, 2005). By designing and building its own RPGs, PIRA could adapt the weapons to its needs as a clandestine organization. Because PIRA could obtain only a limited number of RPGs from international arms sources, group members fleeing the scene of an attack had to carry away the cumbersome launchers, which made them easier to identify and apprehend. By building their own RPGs, the group could make the launchers disposable, facilitating escape after an operation (Jackson, 2005).

Capitalizing on New Opportunities

Changes in a terrorist group's security environment or theater of operations can provide new opportunities. However, even recognizing that a new opportunity exists may require successful information gathering and interpretative processes. Once aware of the potential for a new target or operation, a terrorist group must learn to acquire the capabilities required to exploit it. For example, Hizballah identified and capitalized on the Israeli targets abroad as potential attack sites, expanding beyond its traditional area of operation (Cragin, 2005). The Tamil Tigers—Liberation Tigers of Tamil Eelam (LTTE)—an innovative terrorist insurgency fighting the government of Sri Lanka, developed a range of new attack opportunities through aggressive learning processes; for example, the group exploited key opportunities to strike Sri Lankan naval vessels. Using its knowledge of the navy's tactics and practices, LTTE developed a novel combination of swarming tactics with "wolf hunter packs" of many small boats and a suicide boat packed with explosives to corner and destroy naval patrol vessels (Gunaratna, 2001b).

Improving Skills with Current Weapons or Tactics

> "The difference between the impact of an operation executed well and that of an operation executed poorly can be considerable. . . . In some cases, the price of failure in terrorist operations goes well beyond ineffectiveness."

Although carrying out a terrorist operation seldom requires tactical perfection, the difference between the impact of an operation executed well and that of an operation executed poorly can be considerable. At a minimum, poorly executed operations damage a terrorist group's image as an effective military organization and reduce its chances of presenting the level of threat necessary to achieve its goals. Attacks that are staged particularly poorly can result in even more serious consequences: An attack that kills too many people, strikes the wrong target, or occurs at an inopportune time may trigger high-intensity responses that damage the group, derail other ongoing organizational efforts, or poison all popular support for the group's activities and agenda.

The potential impact of JI's Christmas Eve bombing operation in 2000 was limited because almost half of the 38 devices it used did not detonate (International Crisis Group, 2003; Ressa, 2003). In some cases, the price of failure in terrorist operations goes well beyond ineffectiveness: With explosive devices, for example, the cost of incompetence can be injury and death. The price of such failures has been significant for some terrorist groups. Early in PIRA's operational career, more of its members were killed by their own bombs than by the British Army (Bell, 1998b, p. 392). JI similarly lost members to premature detonations of its explosive devices (International Crisis Group, 2003; Turnbull, 2003).

A terrorist group with the ability to learn can lessen the probability that it will have to pay such high prices. It can evaluate the effectiveness of its activities and take actions to improve its ability to carry them out. In doing so, it not only reduces the chances that its operations will go badly, it can also build significant expertise within the group, enabling it to carry out increasingly complex attacks. Through a variety of learning measures, including learning by doing, use of training to raise the skills of members and reduce the chance of mistakes, and carrying out "after-action reviews" to learn from past failures, all the case study groups were able to increase their levels of effectiveness significantly. JI substantially improved the reliability of its bombing operations after the poorly executed Christmas Eve bombings (Baker, 2005). PIRA's improvement in explosives design and use greatly reduced the group's own fatalities per bombing operation over time (Jackson, 2005).

Effective learning efforts also enable terrorist organizations to cultivate high levels of expertise in critical areas such as bomb making, sniper operations, intelligence gathering, and logistical activities. Internal experts give a terrorist group the potential to significantly advance its level of technological sophistication.[2] PIRA and JI relied on master bombmakers to supply their needs. These bombmakers built up their expertise in constructing explosive devices through constant learning by doing and experimentation. This concentration of talent allowed PIRA to develop standardized bomb "timer and power units" that incorporated necessary safety features and capabilities (Geraghty, 2000; Glover, 1978; Jackson, 2005).

Similarly, Hizballah formed expert units to carry out specific functions. The learning activities of such units could be focused, enabling their members to achieve significantly higher levels of expertise.[3] Before such units were formed, groups for special tasks were drawn from the inner circle around the terrorist group's leadership. While this enabled desired operations to be carried out, it did not allow broad improvement in group capabilities. The transition to relying on specialized units promoted broader group learning in specific areas, such as the use of Ketusha rockets (Cragin, 2005).

Collecting and Utilizing Intelligence Information

> "The quality of the intelligence available to a group can mean the difference between success and failure."

Terrorist groups depend on having access to the right intelligence—knowing where, when, and how to stage an operation for best effect. The quality of the intelligence available to a terrorist group can mean the difference between success and failure. When a group is able to gather good intelligence, it can more

---

[2] Although concentration allows the development of higher levels of expertise, it also involves vulnerabilities. This is discussed in more detail in subsequent chapters.

[3] LTTE is also reported to have adopted specialized units within its group structure. These units include a naval force, an airborne group, special forces units, an intelligence service, and a suicide wing (Chalk, 2000).

readily identify potential targets, locate their vulnerabilities, and understand the security measures intended to protect them. The right kinds of intelligence can also provide information to guide terrorist groups' strategy development and inform them on how law enforcement and intelligence organizations and the public are reacting and responding to the groups' operations. Intelligence can be obtained incidentally—"filtering up without a real system" (Bell, 1998b, p. 472)—but such opportunistic intelligence is not sufficient for consistent effectiveness. Consequently, many groups make intelligence gathering a very high priority and develop specific learning processes and systems for this purpose.

In preparing for specific operations, many terrorist groups have standardized approaches for ensuring that the right information is gathered. The intelligence processes of the case study groups focus on identifying attractive targets and discerning vulnerabilities that can be exploited. Reflecting the common needs of clandestine organizations planning violent operations, groups as different as JI and the ELF/ALF terrorist movement describe common methods of collecting preattack intelligence, including video and photographic surveillance (*White Paper: The Jemaah Islamiyah Arrests and the Threat of Terrorism,* 2003, p. 28(fn); Gunaratna, 2002, pp. 188–189; Leader and Probst, 2003, p. 42).

Many terrorist groups maintain networks of individuals to feed information back into the organization. These groups frequently develop sources within the government and security agencies that oppose them, either by infiltrating them or by recruiting operatives who are already members of those agencies. PIRA used such access to gather information on security forces' activities and to obtain the names of members of law enforcement, intelligence, and military organizations to target for attack (Harnden, 2000; Jackson, 2005). ELF/ALF "members" seek to infiltrate targeted organizations in order to collect information on the organizations' security measures and to collect "evidence" of their environmentally damaging activities for use in postattack propaganda (Hendley and Wegelian, 1993). Hizballah and PIRA collect intelligence on the tactics of the security forces that oppose them and their reactions in specific situations (Cragin, 2005; Harnden, 2000, p. 199). This has allowed the terrorist groups to design specific operations that anticipated and exploited the security forces' own tactics, increasing the effectiveness and lethality of the terrorists' attacks.

Intelligence can also sometimes provide terrorist groups with public relations victories. In the 1970s, PIRA obtained and publicized a top-secret British military assessment of the group that concluded that PIRA "could not be defeated" (Coogan, 1993, p. 283); this bit of intelligence obviously benefited the group's morale.

Because of the importance of being able to gather necessary intelligence, the case study groups devoted considerable effort to maintaining and improving their ability to do so.[4] To build their organizations' capabilities, several terrorist groups included specific intelligence training in their members' regimen and covered the topic in their organizational operations manuals. LTTE, a group with a reputation for the effectiveness of its intelligence activities, reportedly carries out specific after-action reviews of operational successes and failures to strengthen this particular learning activity (Gunaratna, 2001a).

Thwarting Efforts to Combat Terrorist Activities

> "Effective learning makes it more likely that terrorist organizations will be able to overcome the actions aimed at defeating them."

Viewed from a learning-centered perspective, a central goal in combating terrorism is to change the environment of the terrorist group, making its current knowledge and capabilities obsolete. Security measures seek to make available weapons ineffective. Intelligence and law enforcement operations seek to circumvent groups' security measures, thereby compromising members and degrading group capabilities. Effective learning makes it more likely that terrorist organizations will be able to overcome the actions aimed at defeating them.

Terrorist groups undertake a range of defensive counterintelligence and operational security measures to protect themselves. PIRA has used everything from basic measures such as posted lookouts beating trash-can lids as warnings to sophisticated electronic surveillance and compromising security forces' communications systems (Bell, 1998a, pp. 197–198; Foreign and Commonwealth Office, Republic of Ireland Department, 1972; Urban, 1992, pp. 113–114). By giving the terrorist group a window on security force actions, such learning efforts allowed PIRA to move operatives, carry out logistical tasks, and initiate operations more safely. In response to infiltration by security forces that resulted in the compromise of terrorist group operations and the arrest of group members, some groups have made significant modifications to their structures and activities. Both PIRA and Hizballah restructured themselves to institutionalize lessons they learned about protecting themselves from infiltration.[5]

Terrorist groups have also made significant tactical changes to counter security forces' ability to capitalize on vulnerabilities they created. For example, although Hizballah acquired tube-launched, optically tracked, wire-guided (TOW) antitank

---

[4] The importance of terrorist groups' capabilities in intelligence activities emphasizes the role that state sponsors can play in transferring this type of knowledge. Hizballah benefited from intelligence training from Iran early in its operational development, training that strengthened the group's ability to carry out key functions (Cragin, 2005). Analogous assistance was reportedly provided to the Tamil Tigers by the Indian Intelligence Service (Davis, 1996).

[5] Basque Fatherland and Liberty (ETA) reportedly undertook a similar reorganization to increase its security and resilience to security pressures and other countermeasures (Tucker, 2001, p. 139).

missiles and training in how to use them from its state sponsors, using the missiles the way they were taught created significant vulnerabilities for the group. Instead of using the TOW missiles from open areas exposed to rapid counterattack, Hizballah had to learn on its own and develop doctrine for using them in more concealed or defensible areas (Susser, 2000). To counter law enforcement's ability to gather information on them and their members, PIRA and components of the ELF/ALF movements both developed strategies to limit the evidence left behind at operations, including practices directly aimed at countering forensic science investigation methods and the use of secondary devices to destroy residual evidence (Chalk, 2001; Geraghty, 2000; Long and Denson, 1999; workshop discussions).[6]

Successful learning is also critical for circumventing technologies aimed at reducing the attack capabilities of terrorist groups or compromising their security. In PIRA's multidecade conflict in Northern Ireland, a key focus of security force activities was the discovery and prevention of detonation of the bombs that were a central part of the terrorist group's arsenal. The development of countermeasures to remotely detonated explosives triggered successive rounds of innovation by PIRA to break through the defensive measures (Collins and McGovern, 1998; Geraghty, 2000; Glover, 1978). Similar measure-countermeasure interactions occurred in other case study groups as well. For example, use of metal detectors to identify trees that had been "spiked" by ELF members[7] led the terrorist group to utilize spikes that were not made of metal.[8] This adaptation reconstituted the group's ability to use the spiking tactic.

Preserving Organizational Capabilities Despite the Loss of Group Members

The nature of terrorist groups' activities involves risk to individual members. When supporting or carrying out violence, there is always the potential that individuals will be killed or apprehended and the knowledge and expertise they carry will be lost to their organization. Therefore, the ability of a terrorist group to truly carry out *organizational* learning—where capabilities are shared or stored in such a way that they are

---

[6] PIRA efforts to prevent law enforcement information-gathering activities included the extreme strategy of directly attacking the police forensic science laboratory (Geraghty, 2000, p. 90).

[7] To make the trees dangerous to harvest in logging operations.

[8] See, for example, Foreman and Haywood, 1989.

less vulnerable to the loss of specific individuals—can significantly increase the group's level of effectiveness.[9,10]

> "When supporting or carrying out violence, there is always the potential that individuals will be killed or apprehended and the knowledge and expertise they carry will be lost to their organization."

PIRA's pursuit of anti-aircraft missiles provides a ready example of the damage that the loss of a particular person can do to a terrorist group. In its efforts to develop missiles that would be effective against the helicopters frequently used by security forces in Northern Ireland and that it could manufacture itself, PIRA relied on an American engineer to develop the needed technologies. However, the effort was compromised and the engineer was arrested before the work was completed, so the early results were lost (Harnden, 2000, pp. 353–373).

Not all technical capabilities are so vulnerable. Gabriel Cleary, PIRA director of engineering and "the man most responsible for its range of very effective homemade weaponry—from mortars to sophisticated long delay timing devices" (O'Callaghan, 1999, p. 305), was captured during a failed arms-importation attempt in 1987. In that case, the group's technical knowledge in these areas was clearly held more broadly than by Cleary alone. In the five years Cleary was in prison (Mac Dermott, 1998), the organization continued to introduce new generations of increasingly effective mortars (Geraghty, 2000). In 1992, Hizballah lost its leader to an Israeli attack. Although the loss did result in a struggle for control of the group, it did not appear to result in decreased capability (Hirshberg, 1992).

To institutionalize knowledge that would maintain group capabilities, all of the case study groups carried out training programs to distribute knowledge among their members.[11,12] Training of group members can be carried out through a variety of

---

[9] Groups that utilize suicide terrorism present an extreme example of this problem. Since, by definition, the individuals involved in suicide operations cannot return to the group as repositories of knowledge, the group must build an auxiliary organizational structure to capture knowledge related to use of the tactic.

[10] In his study of left-wing groups active in Europe, Pluchinsky examines the ability of these "fighting communist organizations" to reconstitute after significant arrests of their leadership. Such reconstitution is a key test of the effectiveness of an organization's knowledge storage mechanisms—and of whether those mechanisms are truly organizational in nature. Two of the factors Pluchinsky cites as important to this ability—the presence of active members in prisons and a dedicated circle of supporters and sympathizers—could be viewed as storage mechanisms of those organizations (Pluchinsky, 1992, pp. 40–42).

[11] Student notebooks from a training program for Islamic *jihadists* in Uzbekistan provide a detailed description of such a training program (Olcott and Babajanov, 2003).

[12] It should be noted that training efforts and other modes of institutionalizing knowledge within terrorist groups play important roles in transmitting political and ideological information to group members as well. Use of group publications to provide the organization's interpretation of world events and information on group actions and appropriate member activities and behavior is important for maintaining group cohesion and morale. Many terrorist organizations now produce internal publications, an activity greatly facilitated by the development of the Internet.

mechanisms: individuals can be brought together in formal training camps in a range of locations for direct instruction; smaller-scale instruction can be carried out individually or in small groups in safe house locations; and individuals can be trained virtually though transmission of information and interaction via information technology and the Internet. Even ELF/ALF, whose organizational model of leaderless resistance makes any coordinated or centralized actions very difficult, reportedly uses large group gatherings of environmental activists to undertake certain types of training efforts (Trujillo, 2005).

Development of manuals, gaining access to manuals from external sources, and other types of codified knowledge are prominent strategies used by many terrorist organizations to institutionalize group capabilities. The ability of terrorist groups to exchange codified knowledge sources with current members, new and potential recruits, and sympathizers rapidly and securely via the Internet has opened up many new ways for groups to use such information. However, preparation of manuals involves obvious security risks to clandestine groups. Terrorist groups' efforts in this area are known only because the manuals have been seized and their contents compromised. Beyond simply accepting this risk, some terrorist groups (more specifically, movements seeking to inspire terrorist acts by individuals or small groups, including ELF/ALF) have simply made such manuals publicly available through open publication or dissemination on the Internet. In this way, the groups have tried to maintain a level of capability in a network of affiliated groups that is robust to the involvement of many different, potentially quite inexperienced members (Trujillo, 2005).

CHAPTER FOUR

How Understanding Terrorist Group Learning Can Aid in Combating Terrorism

Terrorist groups present a moving target that can prove very difficult to hit. Effectively aiming efforts intended to combat terrorism hinges on being able to anticipate how groups are evolving over time. *Describing* a terrorist group's evolution is a first step toward this end, but *understanding* the processes through which the evolution takes place is even more valuable. Knowledge about the processes through which terrorist groups change enables more-educated anticipation of their future behavior, rather than simply projections based on past actions. With such an understanding, law enforcement and intelligence analysts may be able to anticipate where and how a terrorist group is likely to be operating in the future.

The study of organizational learning provides a window onto *how* terrorist groups change and adapt and can contribute to planning and operations for combating terrorism across three phases of activity (see Figure 4.1):[1]

- **Detection.** Improved understanding of terrorist group learning can facilitate detection of their efforts to change.
- **Anticipation.** Understanding of organizational learning can improve the ability to anticipate whether terrorist organizations will be successful in their activities.
- **Action.** Increased understanding strengthens the capability to act against terrorist groups by illuminating the effects of group learning on countermeasures and suggesting novel counterterrorism strategies.

---

[1] Of course, it will never be possible to capture all the elements that determine how terrorist groups evolve. Groups will make random or unpremeditated changes, organizational factors and psychology will skew their decisionmaking, and circumstances will influence them in ways that cannot be foreseen (McCormick, 2003).

Figure 4.1
Phases of Law Enforcement and Intelligence Activity to Counter Terrorist Group Efforts to Change and Adapt

RAND *MG331-4.1*

Detecting Terrorist Groups' Efforts to Change

In hindsight, organizational learning in a terrorist group is usually easy to detect. It is clear that PIRA learned in the process of transforming its organizational structures to address security needs (Jackson, 2005). It is similarly clear that Aum Shinrikyo learned in order to synthesize the sarin it used on the Tokyo subway (Parachini, 2005). But detecting a terrorist group's efforts to change *before* the changes are fully realized and used in an attack is much less straightforward. This is where an understanding of the *process* of learning—and subsequent change and adaptation—can be invaluable.[2] As summarized in Figure 4.2, this understanding can help

- *Guide intelligence collection* by identifying the appropriate information to gather
- *Contribute to intelligence analysis* by ensuring that critical data are not overlooked and by guiding interpretation of intelligence information

Equipped with these insights, analysts stand a much better chance of recognizing and correctly interpreting signals that indicate learning is taking place while it is still taking place, rather than after it has been successfully completed.

Guidance for Intelligence Collection

For the intelligence analyst examining an individual terrorist organization, the questions, "Is the terrorist group learning and, if so, how?" are clearly important. To

---

[2] The need to detect and understand terrorist organizations' efforts to change has been appreciated throughout the history of terrorist violence. Some indicators of terrorist group learning have therefore been available for some time; for example, law enforcement and intelligence analysts have long tracked indicators of weapons procurement by terrorist groups and attempts by groups to gain access to key technical capabilities. However, in the absence of a clear and comprehensive framework for understanding group learning, there are no guarantees that currently available indicators are sufficient. It is apparent from the analyses of our five case study groups that the available indicators tell only part of the story.

Figure 4.2
Understanding Group Learning to Aid in Detection

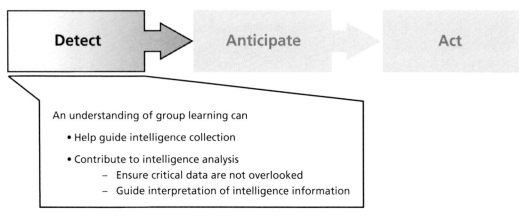

An understanding of group learning can

- Help guide intelligence collection

- Contribute to intelligence analysis
    - Ensure critical data are not overlooked
    - Guide interpretation of intelligence information

RAND *MG331-4.2*

answer them, the analyst must have access to the right information. However, there is no guarantee that all the information needed will be collected, since simply asking whether or not a terrorist group is learning provides little guidance on the specific information that must be collected to find an answer. To apply an analogy of assembling a jigsaw puzzle to intelligence analysis, while the question may describe the picture we want to see when the puzzle is finished, it does not provide any guidance about where we should look to find individual puzzle pieces. In effect, the question, "Is a terrorist group learning?" is not "actionable" from the perspective of intelligence collection because of the complexity inherent in the process of organizational learning.

> "By breaking out the component processes required for organizational learning, the framework enables one to identify the intelligence that must be collected to detect and understand groups' efforts to learn and adapt."

In contrast, the individual components of organizational learning—information gathering, interpretation, distribution, and storage—are sufficiently specific and distinct to suggest actionable questions. Focusing on a specific component, such as how a terrorist group is gathering the information needed to support its learning effort, leads to a range of questions about the group's knowledge sources and how it is developing or importing new information or knowledge.[3] Because the elements of the

---

[3] Focusing intelligence and investigation resources on the specific components of a terrorist group's organizational learning process can produce significant successes in efforts to combat terrorism. When they were investigating changes in PIRA's advanced bomb detonators, security forces in Northern Ireland focused on the nature of the knowledge sources that the group needed to develop the technologies. By tracing back through the source of specific electronic components of the bombs, the police identified an American engineer who was providing tech-

learning process suggest much more specific questions to ask, they can help the intelligence collector locate individual pieces of the puzzle describing a terrorist group's learning efforts. By breaking out the component processes required for organizational learning, the framework enables one to identify the intelligence that must be collected to detect and understand groups' efforts to learn and adapt (workshop discussions; see also Cragin and Daly, 2004, pp. 57–59).

Because successful organizational learning requires a terrorist group to carry out all four of the component processes described in Chapter Two, the analyst requires information on all of them to fully understand the group's adaptive efforts. When pieces of the puzzle are missing—when the analyst has data on only one or two of the individual processes—it can be impossible to fully understand terrorist group learning. Each of our case studies revealed significant disparities in the amount of information available, at least in the open literature, on these four processes. For example, while knowledge-gathering activities[4] have received significant emphasis, much less attention has been devoted to interpretation. The available literature is largely silent about how the case study terrorist groups made decisions about activities, tactics, or technologies to pursue; how they judged the success or failure of their activities; and how those judgments affected their behavior.[5] The processes of distribution and storage, where knowledge becomes broadly available to the group rather than held only by certain key individuals, have also been underemphasized.[6]

This suggests that law enforcement, intelligence, and other counterterrorist planners might encounter important "blind spots" as they attempt to analyze information that will enable them to understand terrorist group-learning processes.[7] By providing a systematic approach to defining what information must be collected to understand group learning, the four-part organizational learning model can help ensure that such blind spots are addressed. This approach could require as little effort as

---

nical assistance to the terrorist group. That same individual was also helping the group develop technologies to build antiaircraft missiles whose deployment would have significantly changed the nature of the conflict. By successfully getting inside the terrorist group's learning processes, the police were able to disrupt that effort before it was successful (Harnden, 2000; Jackson, 2005).

[4] These activities include terrorist groups' efforts to obtain weapons or recruit specific technical experts.

[5] Though the scarcity of information on such "internal" processes is not surprising, getting access to such information is obviously critical for fully understanding decisionmaking by terrorist groups in their learning efforts.

[6] Although it was not the primary focus of this research effort, workshop participants emphasized that understanding the individual components of the learning framework could also enable development of clearer intelligence-collection goals, i.e., the specific types of information that are most useful for detecting terrorist group activities and learning efforts. In an era where intelligence collection, particularly in the U.S. homeland, relies on information collected by a wide range of organizations—federal, state, local, and even the private sector—standardized goals could make an important contribution to improving the collection of critical information.

[7] This suggestion assumes, to some extent, that the information available in the open literature broadly reflects what is available in classified sources. Though this will certainly not be the case in many areas, workshop participants indicated that it may be generally appropriate for other areas or groups.

asking additional questions about a terrorist group's efforts to learn, either during routine intelligence-gathering efforts or during focused activities such as interrogation of captured group members. To the extent that terrorist groups have broadly established strategies and practices underlying their learning activities, the answers to these questions could provide durable insights into how groups go about their efforts to change.

Contribution to Intelligence Analysis

"Analysts need analytical frameworks into which to place acquired data. . . . An understanding of terrorist group learning provides an important additional framework for assessing intelligence information."

The model of the organizational learning process can also help intelligence and law enforcement analysts analyze information that has been collected. Every day, analysts receive a huge influx of intelligence data. Knowing what pieces of that intelligence are most important and how to make sense of new information in the context of what is already known about a terrorist group is not always straightforward. Analysts need analytical frameworks into which to place acquired data and to help make judgments about the relative importance of individual pieces of information (Libicki and Pfleeger, 2004). Such frameworks help to

- Ensure that critical data points are not overlooked
- Assist in determining what intelligence information means and how important it is with respect to overall group structures and activities

Many such frameworks are based, for example, on assumptions about terrorist groups' strategic goals, member psychology, or organizational dynamics (see, for example, McCormick, 2003). An understanding of terrorist group learning provides an important additional framework for assessing intelligence information.

Ensuring That Critical Intelligence Data Are Not Overlooked

A model of organizational learning can help single out information related to a group's efforts to change, such as how the group gathers or stores information. Without the framework such a model provides, signals related to learning could easily slip by unnoticed. To minimize the chance of this happening, characteristic indicators of terrorist group learning activities could be developed to point directly to possible red flags. Detecting one of these indicators could cue an analyst to significant changes in learning efforts within a known group and could even help to identify early indicators of malevolent activity within a group that has not yet been identified. In the PIRA case, for example, experimentation during the development of several different weapons resulted in explosions in remote areas where the group was

> "A systematic understanding of group learning . . . helps to ensure that information on different types of group learning activities will not be overlooked."

conducting engineering and testing activities (Jackson, 2005). These were relatively unambiguous signs that learning was taking place. Aum Shinrikyo's efforts to develop biological weapons led people living near the cult's facilities to report strange smells and emissions to environmental agencies; these were also signals that the group was learning, although they were not appreciated as such at the time (Parachini, 2005). Indicators of other types of learning-related activities could similarly be applied to different weapons or operational areas.

A systematic understanding of terrorist group learning processes, coupled with an understanding of what and how a group needs to learn based on the environment in which it operates,[8] can also help to ensure that information on different *types* of group learning activities will not be overlooked. For example, an analyst who, because of concerns about major changes in a group's operations, focuses only on its potential for discontinuous learning, might miss important data on continuous improvement activities. A terrorist group learning gradually over time might draw on different information or knowledge sources, use different criteria for interpretation, and distribute and store knowledge in different ways than it would if it were aiming to make a rapid shift in its strategies or operations. Moreover, a succession of incremental changes over time could eventually demonstrate the need for and catalyze more discontinuous change; if such changes were not monitored, the subsequent transformation could come as a surprise.

Assisting the Analyst in Determining What Intelligence Data Mean

An analytical framework describing a terrorist group's organizational learning efforts can also help law enforcement and intelligence analysts understand the meaning of information about a terrorist group. Such a framework can provide both

> "An analytical framework describing a group's organizational learning efforts can also help law enforcement and intelligence analysts understand the meaning of information about a terrorist group."

- A better context for a group's current activities by *looking back* into the group's learning history
- A more complete understanding of a group's operations by *looking forward* at the full learning implications of its current activities

---

[8] An understanding of a group's learning requirements for its environment and desired change would need to be developed through techniques such as red-teaming and analysis of scenarios a group might pursue under different conditions.

Looking back, the model can make it easier for analysts to interpret a terrorist group's current learning activities in the context of its learning history. The way a group carried out the four component processes in past situations provides a context for interpreting new information about its activities. For example, PIRA had a long history of developing and manufacturing new weapons systems such as RPGs and mortar systems. Therefore, it is not surprising that when the group sought to acquire antiaircraft missiles, it wanted to manufacture them internally as well (Harnden, 2000, pp. 353–373). How PIRA went about learning in the past suggested how it might do so in the present and future.

Looking forward, examining a terrorist group's actions from the viewpoint of how the group learns also provides an alternative framework for understanding the meaning and implications of its activities. A specific action, such as recruiting members in a new area or country, is given meaning by the analytical framework applied when the analyst integrates it into an overall picture of what a terrorist group is doing. In a framework assessing the group's strategic goals, such an act might be interpreted as an expansion of violent activities into the new country. In a framework assessing behavior with respect to the psychology and internal dynamics of an organization, the same act might be interpreted as reflecting the group's need to appear dynamic to support the morale of its current membership. The meaning of an act can be interpreted very differently, depending on the nature of the framework imposed upon it by the analyst. Although such interpretation is an essential part of the intelligence analysis process, if the frameworks applied are inappropriate or incomplete, the analyst could seriously misinterpret the implications of a terrorist group's actions.

Without an analytical framework that captures a terrorist group's learning activities, an analyst may not be able to appreciate the learning implications of the group's actions. In contrast to the above interpretations of recruiting in a new country, from a learning perspective, such activity might indicate information or knowledge gathering aimed at building a new capability or acquiring a new tactic. Similarly, specific attacks that do not make sense from a strategic perspective may be perfectly reasonable from a learning perspective. For example, if a terrorist group attacks a target that seems to have low priority or is outside its usual areas of operation, an analysis focused on strategy might conclude that the group has been forced away from its favored targets or has shifted its goals. But from a learning perspective, such an attack could be seen quite differently, perhaps as an important "dress rehearsal" to help the group learn what it needs to do to carry out a higher-profile operation in the future.[9]

---

[9] As an example, Harnden suggests that a PIRA attack on a security forces base in November 1984 using a single mortar tube was a rehearsal staged to test out a generation of the technologies and to help determine firing ranges

Other actions may also have learning implications along with the other benefits they provide to a terrorist group. Using a learning-focused model to examine intelligence can help ensure that those implications are not missed. State sponsorship of terrorism is an example. The potential contributions that state sponsors can make to terrorist groups through activities such as military training and provision of weapons, sanctuary, and intelligence have long been appreciated (see, for example, Byman et al., 2001). However, focusing on the full range of potential impacts that such sponsorship can have on group learning provides a more complete picture of these activities. For example, Hizballah's connections to state sponsorship had two specific learning effects that, to our knowledge, are underappreciated. First, Iran's provision of intelligence training was important for building Hizballah's internal capacity to learn. Without outside help, the group would have had to build that capability on its own and might not have done so effectively. Second, beyond the direct benefits a terrorist group can receive from a sponsor, it is also important that such support can "free up" group resources that can then be applied to other learning activities. This effect is demonstrated by comparing the situation faced by Hizballah with that of PIRA. When Hizballah encountered problems with its weapons—e.g., jamming of its radio detonators—it simply obtained new, more effective weapons from its sponsors. When PIRA found itself in a similar position, it had to devote learning resources to adapting the technologies on its own. By freeing up some of the group's "learning budget," sponsorship allowed Hizballah to learn more effectively in other areas (Cragin, 2005).

Anticipating the Outcome of Terrorist Groups' Efforts to Change

> "Threat is not just about what a terrorist group wants to do or tries to do; threat is based on what it can do successfully."

It is always worrisome when a terrorist group decides to acquire new weapons or adopt a new tactic. But whether or not such a decision actually increases the threat the group poses depends on whether it can bring its plans to fruition. Threat is not just about what a terrorist group wants to do or tries to do; threat is based on what it can do it successfully. In fact, if a group's attempt at learning is unsuccessful, the decision to learn something new might actually decrease its level of threat by pulling group resources away from other activities it

for the February 28, 1985, attack on the police station at Newry. The Newry attack involved nine such weapons and claimed the lives of nine police officers (Harnden, 2000, pp. 232–234).

could carry out successfully.[10] A sufficiently ineffective attempt to learn could compromise or even injure or kill group members, reducing the group's ability to carry out future attacks.

To design measures to combat terrorism and to effectively allocate scarce intelligence or law enforcement resources, it is necessary to assess the threat a variety of adversaries pose as accurately as possible. The ability to do so requires more than information about intent, since many groups intend to do far more than they will ever be able to actually accomplish.

A terrorist group's ability to learn determines its chance of success. Learning is the link between what a group wants to do and its ability to bring together the information and resources to actually do it. Consequently, understanding how terrorist groups learn can directly contribute to the ability to anticipate whether their actions will be successful and, accordingly, to determine the level of threat they pose.

Two complementary strategies, one focused on the terrorist group and the other on what it is trying to do, can help provide the insight needed to better anticipate a terrorist group's chance of success by

- Singling out characteristics of terrorist groups and their circumstances that are useful in assessing whether they are likely to be strong or weak learners
- Identifying what information, expertise, and other capabilities are required for a group's learning activities to be successful so that analysts can more effectively assess its efforts

The contribution of understanding organizational learning to the ability to anticipate a group's chance of being successful is summarized in Figure 4.3.

Identifying Characteristics of Terrorist Groups and Circumstances That Affect Learning[11]

An understanding of the processes of organizational learning can help identify the characteristics that are important to the success of a terrorist group's efforts to adapt and change. Previous studies of organizational learning in many types of organizations have identified a variety of characteristics associated with specific groups' abili-

---

[10] Concern about chemical, biological, radiological, and nuclear weapons falling into the hands of terrorist groups provides a ready example. Although pursuit of such weapons by any terrorist group should raise concerns, the intent to acquire them may not increase—and could actually decrease—the real threat the group poses to either specific targets or the public at large if it cannot learn how to gain possession of the weapons and to use them successfully.

[11] Gerwehr and Glenn (2003, pp. 49–53) describe a complementary set of characteristics combining both group propensity to change and elements included in this discussion relating to a group's likelihood of changing successfully.

Figure 4.3
Understanding Group Learning to Aid in Anticipation

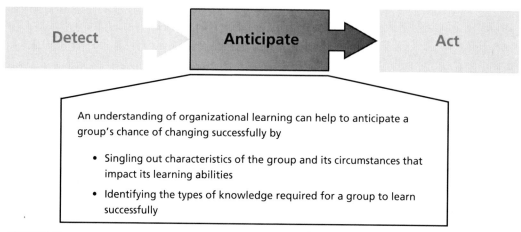

An understanding of organizational learning can help to anticipate a group's chance of changing successfully by

- Singling out characteristics of the group and its circumstances that impact its learning abilities
- Identifying the types of knowledge required for a group to learn successfully

RAND *MG331-4.3*

ties to learn effectively.[12] These characteristics assist in describing the nature of an organization's structure and interconnections, membership, and activities and how each affects the ability of an organization to learn effectively.

The following sections describe eight characteristics (shown in Figure 4.4) that are useful in describing the nature of terrorist groups vis-à-vis their learning efforts. Because of the number of characteristics that have been identified as potentially influencing the ability of groups to learn, these descriptions are comparatively brief and do not comprehensively examine all elements of the characteristics' effects on group learning.[13] The examples presented are intended to illustrate the relevance of each characteristic for assessing the learning capabilities of terrorist organizations. We have not attempted to calibrate their relative impact on specific groups' learning capabilities.[14]

---

[12] See, for example, Jackson, 2001; Trujillo and Jackson, forthcoming, and references therein.

[13] For example, studies of group structure have assessed not only the learning impact of the overall structure of organizations (e.g., hierarchy, network, team organization, etc.), but also the specific ways work teams within an organization are structured and how organizational design affects activities down to the level of interactions between individuals (see, for example, Hong, 1999). Completely exploring terrorist group structure would require examining both the relevance and impact of the full range of variables on group operations. The intent of this study was to provide a survey of organizational learning in a range of terrorist groups, and such detailed examination was beyond the scope of the project.

[14] More-quantitative characterization of each group trait and its specific (and cumulative) impacts on group learning would require additional study across a wider and more broadly representative sample of terrorist organizations.

Figure 4.4
Characteristics That Affect Terrorist Group Learning Abilities

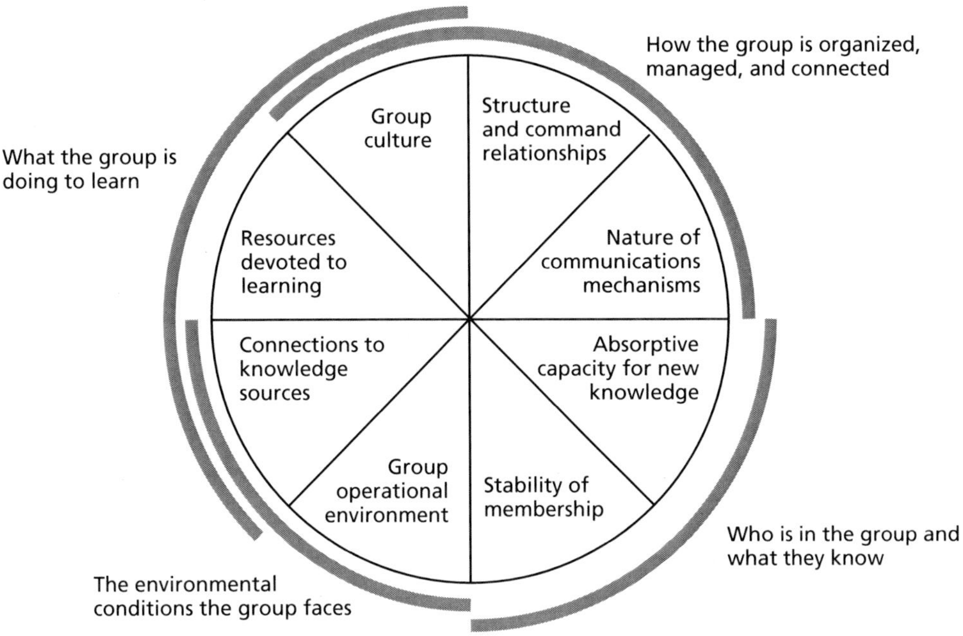

RAND *MG331-4.4*

Structure and Command Relationships

An organization's internal structure can significantly affect its ability to learn. There are many different variations of possible group structures, from classic hierarchical "management trees," where a group leader manages activities through multiple layers of organizational units, to hub-and-spoke networks, where a central commander controls many individual units, to less-structured "leaderless resistance," or "all-channel," networks, where a group lacks a central management function, but activities are coordinated through communications among all individual units (see Arquilla and Ronfeldt, 2001, for a discussion of group structures and terrorist groups).

Previous research has identified a range of potential impacts of group structure on organizational learning. For example, requirements to transmit information and knowledge through many layers of a group's command structure can impede learning if information is lost as it is distributed or if communications can no longer take place.[15] Within terrorist groups, such communications can also represent a signifi-

---

[15] A statement by Patrizio Peci, a leader of the Red Brigades, illustrates this particularly well: "When there are few in the group, there are even discussions on how to move about in the street, what sort of clothes are best used. The mistakes leading to the capture of comrades are studied, there is much discussion. When the organization

cant security risk. These tradeoffs emphasize the dual impacts of a group's size on learning capability: While a larger number of individuals can increase capability, it can also increase the need for management structures and processes. The nature of a terrorist group's structure can also influence the vulnerability of the organization's memory and stored knowledge to deterioration, depending on how compartmentalized particular types of knowledge are in different components of the group (Carley, 1992; see also Hong, 1999). The difficulties of effective communications and failures in organizational memory can both hinder a group's ability to learn.

The security vulnerabilities and inefficiencies in communications inherent in many group structures have led some terrorist groups to shift their structural models to improve their learning performance. PIRA and Hizballah created specialized internal units that focused on particular activities such as intelligence, specific attack forms, and logistical functions. This structural shift increased the terrorist groups' effectiveness by focusing learning efforts within the specialized functions. Grouping similar specialists together allows deeper learning and sharing of expertise, while minimizing the need to distribute information or knowledge broadly.[16]

The level of control and command authority exerted through the relationships among different parts of an organization can also significantly affect ability to learn. Our five case studies provide a number of examples of how command authority exercised through groups' management structures can affect this ability. Combinations of group structures and command relationships that allow individual units significant autonomy provide considerable opportunities to experiment and innovate at the tactical level. In PIRA, for example, even though a centralized council commanded the group, the council reportedly did not fully control all of the activities of individual cells (Bell, 1998b, pp. 468–469, 591; Collins and McGovern, 1998, p. 220; Drake, 1998, p. 29; O'Doherty, 1993). This allowed different parts of PIRA to attempt new operations ranging from attacking and sinking British coal ships at sea to attempting to bomb security force targets from the air (Jackson, 2005). Such freedom can help overall organizational learning, as the group can choose among the experiments and repeat those it deems useful.

On the other hand, autonomy at the cell level can make it much more difficult for the group to implement a coherent overall strategy. For example, at times, when the overall leadership of PIRA was involved in negotiations or other political activity aimed at advancing the group's agenda by means other than violence, individual units carried out attacks, effectively sabotaging the efforts (Bell, 1998b, pp.

---

becomes larger, however, there is less discussion. It seems paradoxical, but it is so. Dealing with a compartmentalized organization, global discussion is almost impossible and, as a result, everyone ends up doing more or less what he wants, even because it becomes more difficult to reach the senior leader" (Peci, 1983, p. 86). We thank Dennis Pluchinsky for bringing this example to our attention.

[16] The Revolutionary Armed Forces of Colombia (FARC) (Ortiz, 2002) and the Tamil Tigers (Chalk, 2000) have also reportedly adopted this strategy.

468–469).[17] Granting cells autonomy can also undermine a group's ability to learn at the strategic level, i.e., to shape the totality of its operations and activities to improve its chances of achieving broader group goals. Strategic learning requires that a group make changes in the types of operations it pursues or the ways it pursues them and then determine which changes are beneficial and which hurt the group's interests. If individual units do not respond to central coordination, it is difficult or impossible to gather the information needed to improve a group's strategy. In contrast, terrorist groups with much tighter command authority and centralized coordination, such as Hizballah (Cragin, 2005), are better able to shape their overall activities and engage in strategic learning.[18]

When considering a terrorist group's learning capabilities, analysts must determine if the group's structure and command relationships will make it easier or more difficult to bring together the needed resources and knowledge. For activities that rely on bringing together significant tacit knowledge, group structures must support the sharing of that knowledge by the right individuals. The formation of specialized units that collocate specialists is one strategy that terrorist groups have utilized. If mostly explicit knowledge is needed for an action, such linkages are less critical. Similarly, terrorist groups seeking to execute complex strategies that require coordination of many elements to achieve the needed learning must have stronger and more centralized command than groups whose focus is on making improvements at the tactical level. Any mismatch between the requirements of what a terrorist group is attempting and the structures it has to support those efforts reduces the chance of success.

The Nature of Group Communications Mechanisms

Whether a group has strong or weak communications capabilities can significantly affect the likelihood of its success in a learning effort. Even if a group has all the knowledge and expertise it needs to carry out a new type of attack, its attempt will fail if the members who have that knowledge cannot communicate reliably. Similarly, if key knowledge cannot be communicated for interpretation and decisionmaking, a group may miss important opportunities or make critical errors (Bell, 1993, pp. 5–6). Furthermore, effective communication among group members is critical in order for knowledge to make the transition from individual knowledge to truly *organizational* knowledge. As a result, in addition to influencing the success of a particular learning effort, communications

---

[17] Examples of similar situations have been cited with respect to the Front for the Liberation of Quebec and the Palestinian Liberation Organization (PLO) (Tucker, 2001, and references therein).

[18] A recent analysis of al Qaeda specifically mentions the difficulty of implementing coherent and effective terrorist group strategies in networked organizations without sufficient control mechanisms (McAllister, 2004).

capabilities strongly influence the robustness of the overall capabilities of an organization.

A group's ability to distribute information and knowledge for interpretation and use depends on both available technological modes of communications—how it communicates—and interpersonal networks among group members—who chooses to communicate with whom (Beeby and Booth, 2000). In terrorist groups, security concerns impose significant additional limits on communications, since compromise of communications paths can provide major opportunities for security forces to act against a group.

Our case studies provide examples of group communications practices ranging from JI's transfer of simple tactical information via cell phones (Baker, 2005) to many groups' extensive training efforts to communicate practical, ideological, and organizational knowledge to new and existing group members.[19] The ability to train and thereby communicate critical explicit and tacit knowledge to members was a key component of all the organizations' efforts to build robust capabilities. Other examples of communications mechanisms that supported organizational learning efforts include maintenance of formal "doctrine development" processes by Hizballah (Cragin, 2005) and the broad use of training manuals by many of the case study organizations. By capturing critical knowledge, such manuals make it easy to transfer knowledge among the entire organization.

Effective transfer of knowledge among group members requires the use of communications modes that are appropriate for the type of information being transferred. Explicit and tacit knowledge require different mechanisms of communications. Tacit knowledge relies much more on direct face-to-face interaction (reviewed in Gertler, 2001), so if security or other pressures force a group to limit such interaction, learning efforts that depend on the transfer of tacit knowledge will suffer.

As an example of this tradeoff, security concerns caused PIRA to shift from a relatively open structure, where many members interacted frequently, to a compartmentalized, cellular one. Although the cellular structure was supposed to significantly restrict communications among members, the transition was described as "incomplete"—connections and exchange of individuals among cells persisted because some types of knowledge still had to be transferred (Jackson, 2005).

The nature of a terrorist group's available communications mechanisms can provide some insight into the likelihood that specific learning efforts will be successful. Strong communications links, such as the ability to train extensively, increase the chance that a group can effectively share the tacit and explicit knowledge needed to build robust group capabilities. However, in thinking about the potential impact a terrorist group's communications can have on its learning efforts, the analyst must

---

[19] Many of these communications mechanisms require a secure territorial haven. This is discussed briefly in the section on terrorist groups' operational environments.

remain cognizant of what the group is trying to accomplish. Though the lack of face-to-face communications capabilities could be a significant impediment to efforts relying on tacit knowledge, other learning efforts could be affected less.

Absorptive Capacity for New Knowledge

Even if a group acquires useful knowledge, it must be able to absorb and apply it or it will not learn and its operations will not benefit. A group's ability to interpret new knowledge and put it to use is largely determined by the relationship between the new knowledge and what the group and its members already know (Hall and Khan, 2003). For example, technologies that are similar to those already in use by the organization are easier to absorb (Gopalakrishnan and Bierly, 2001; Mowery et al., 1996; Robinson et al., 2003) because they require the least changes.[20]

Groups that lack the knowledge necessary to absorb a desired technology must develop that knowledge to succeed. This additional learning requirement can slow a group's effective use of the new technology. When PIRA made its initial attempts to use RPGs, it lacked the necessary knowledge and experience, and as a result, its early attempts were largely ineffective (Bell, 1987, pp. 53–54). Subsequently, the group built up the knowledge needed and put the weapons to more effective use (Jackson, 2005). When Aum decided to produce and use biological weapons, an activity dramatically different from anything the group had done previously, its lack of the knowledge needed to absorb the technologies resulted in multiple failures (Parachini, 2005).[21]

Because of the impact that absorptive capacity can have on a terrorist group's chances of learning successfully, information on the group's previous learning efforts and available knowledge—the primary determinants of that capacity—is important for judging the likely outcomes of future efforts. To the extent that analysts can build an understanding of a target group's ability to absorb related knowledge, their judgments about future innovation will benefit. For example, understanding PIRA's efforts to develop new generations of machined weapons is critical for evaluating its later efforts to design and manufacture antiaircraft missiles (Jackson, 2005). Though missiles are significantly different from RPGs or mortars, developing them would draw on many of the skills the group had developed in its earlier weapons manufacturing efforts and would therefore increase the effort's chances of success. In contrast,

---

[20] Groups that have done similar things in the past will already possess some of the tacit knowledge needed to succeed at the new activity.

[21] To minimize the impacts of absorptive-capacity problems, terrorist groups can use elite and specialized units to introduce and validate new technologies. By building expert units within the organization, a terrorist group can improve its ability to absorb new technologies that are related to the units' areas of expertise. Hizballah and PIRA, as well as the LTTE (Chalk, 2000) and FARC (Ortiz, 2002), built such units within their organizations and gave them prominent roles in learning activities in their areas of expertise.

Aum Shinrikyo devoted much of its learning efforts to unconventional weapons, developing capabilities in technologies related to chemical and biological agents. As a result, any group effort to utilize the plans the group had acquired for manufacturing Russian AK-74 rifles would have had little relevant past experience to support it (Parachini, 2005). An analyst could therefore safely conclude that it would require additional learning efforts on Aum's part if the effort were to be carried out successfully.

Stability of Membership

 A key component of all organizations' memories is the expertise and knowledge held in the minds of their members. Loss of members who hold key knowledge can be a major blow to an organization's ability to learn. Furthermore, continuous improvement efforts, where individual members or units of an organization accumulate knowledge or skill over time, are critical for building expertise. Groups whose membership is stable have greater opportunities to build up expertise gradually and less chance of losing knowledge through the departure of group members (Carley, 1992; Edmonson et al., 2003; Kim, 1993; Lipshitz et al., 2002).[22]

One of PIRA's most stable units was a cell based in South Armagh, a region on the border between Northern Ireland and the Irish Republic. Its members operated together for many years, enabling it to build up a level of capability and military precision that set it apart from the rest of the terrorist organization. The unit was more successful in carrying out operations safely—"there were fewer mistakes and therefore fewer arrests in South Armagh than in any other [PIRA] Brigade area" (Harnden, 2000, p. 46). The unit's expertise also provided PIRA with a key resource for learning: The South Armagh Brigade frequently introduced new weapons and tactics, and it played key roles in supporting high-profile PIRA operations (Harnden, 2000, p. 19). Similarly, because of the long tenure of its members, the inner circle of Hizballah's original command structure, which had knowledge and skills built up over time, was drawn on for high-profile attacks that had significant learning requirements (Cragin, 2005). The long operational experience of individual JI and PIRA bombmakers (although not necessarily the groups' members in general) was vital to the terrorist groups' abilities to improve their explosive devices incrementally over time ("Azahari's Tracks," 2003; Glover, 1978).

Assessing the impact of terrorist group stability on group learning is potentially particularly difficult, since the intelligence necessary to do so will likely be harder to

---

[22] As with many of the other characteristics described in this chapter, the length of terrorist group members' operational careers is a *potential* contributor to improved group learning capability, but it does not immediately and positively follow that an increase in membership stability will result in more-effective learning. Details matter. For example, if members extend their longevity by going underground and do not participate in activities related to group functions for many years, the group's learning capability is unlikely to increase.

obtain. However, any information that can be collected on individual terrorists' tenures and experiences or similar data on particular units within an organization could yield important insights for assessing terrorist group efforts.[23]

The Nature of the Group's Operational Environment

The environment in which any given group operates is perhaps the dominant factor influencing both the group's incentive and its capacity to learn. The environment defines the group's operational opportunities and the types of learning it might pursue to take advantage of them, influences the types of investments it makes in learning, and governs its potential to learn (Dodgson, 1993; Garvin, 1993).

A terrorist group's environment helps shape its learning goals, which in turn determine the kind of learning the group will need to achieve them: Certain environments and goals may call for continuous improvement efforts, while others might favor major changes. Groups that have waged ongoing terrorist-insurgent campaigns in comparatively stable theaters of operation, such as PIRA and Hizballah, carry out many more individual operations than groups that engage in terrorism more episodically, such as JI or Aum. A higher operational tempo provides more opportunities for incremental learning activities, such as refining marksmanship and building better explosives, potentially making highly active terrorist groups much better at continuous improvement.

Efforts to combat terrorism are major sources of uncertainty and threat in a terrorist group's environment. As a result, a group's ability to insulate itself from those pressures and gain the time and opportunity to evaluate new knowledge, modify strategies, and carry out other learning activities is a key determinant of its ability to learn effectively. In our case studies, there appears to be a break point in learning between terrorist groups that were able to gain sufficient safe haven[24] to be able to experiment and innovate away from direct pressure and those that could not.[25] PIRA, Hizballah, and Aum each had the ability to make that space—either literally or figuratively, on their own or with the help of sympathetic states—and as a result, they increased their ability to learn.

Environmental characteristics are readily identifiable influences on a terrorist group's potential to succeed in a specific learning activity. Groups' operational tempo and experience with continuous improvement efforts can provide a clue to potential outcomes. Across all terrorist groups, the importance of safe havens for learning is

---

[23] As both the PIRA and JI cases suggest, these data can sometimes be inferred from the analysis of specific individuals' products—e.g., identifying the tenure of the bombmaker through the signature of his or her workmanship in the bomb.

[24] See Byman et al., 2001, and Cragin and Daly, 2004, for further discussion of safe havens.

[25] See Takeyh and Gvosdev, 2002, for discussion of the role of safe havens in multinational terrorist networks.

clear. Without the safety needed to experiment and test new ideas and operations, a group's chances of implementing them successfully are significantly reduced.

Connections to Knowledge Sources

 Having access to the knowledge needed to carry out desired activities is essential to a group's ability to learn. Connections to appropriate knowledge sources can increase the chance that groups will be able to locate and use necessary information and knowledge (Hardy et al., 2003).

To gain access to explicit knowledge required for group learning efforts—i.e., plans, technologies, weapons—terrorist groups must be connected to the right sources. For example, obtaining weapons and armaments is a key goal of most terrorist groups, so they need to know where and how to get them. PIRA was initially limited in its ability to acquire weapons by its lack of knowledge of how to interact with and draw on the international arms market, a shortfall only partially made up for by arms provided by Libya and sympathetic sources in the United States. To make up for its limited connections to arms sources, PIRA had to undertake the learning efforts required to manufacture its own weapons (Bell, 1998b, p. 373). PIRA's lack of connections to sources of explicit knowledge therefore delayed its acquisition of particular tactics and technologies. In contrast, to procure arms, even beyond those provided by its state sponsors in Iran and Syria, Hizballah built up an extensive international network, including activities in Colombia (Cragin and Hoffman, 2003).

Sources such as the Internet and information in the open literature can provide access to a wide variety of explicit knowledge, including information supporting target selection and attack planning, technical information relevant to weapons and operations, and assistance in connecting to sources of needed supplies or other materiel.

For many group learning efforts, organizations must also have access to people and organizations that possess necessary tacit knowledge. Otherwise, they must develop the knowledge for themselves, which can either slow or defeat their learning efforts. PIRA, Hizballah, JI, and Aum Shinrikyo all effectively connected with outside experts (from state sponsors and other sources) to obtain desired knowledge and capabilities. They also interacted with other terrorist groups to obtain knowledge. For example, JI's ties with al Qaeda provided opportunities for learning about explosives (Baker, 2005; Arquilla and Ronfeldt, 2001).

A terrorist group's connections to knowledge sources are a key element for assessing terrorist group learning capabilities and an organization's likelihood of success in carrying out ongoing attempts to learn. Intelligence training from states and access to individuals with operational military experience were particularly critical for several of the terrorist organizations in our case studies. Terrorist groups that have strong connections to the right sources of knowledge are more likely to be successful.

Resources Devoted to Learning

Although learning can occur as an incidental product of routine operations, groups frequently must devote resources and individuals to achieve it. While many organizations hesitate to commit resources to anything but "direct operations," those willing to devote human and capital resources to learning have a greater chance that a learning effort will be successful.[26] Aum Shinrikyo and PIRA conducted ongoing "research and development" aimed specifically at learning to support their efforts to develop new weapons and acquire novel tactics.[27]

In assessing a terrorist group's potential for success, the analyst must consider the type and level of resources the group has committed to the learning effort. It is important to note, however, that simply committing resources does not guarantee success. Aum Shinrikyo devoted very significant resources to its biological and chemical weapons activities but was ultimately unsuccessful (Leitenberg, 1999; Rosenau, 2001).[28]

Group Culture

A group's culture directly affects its ability to learn. Learning efforts are influenced by systems of reward and reprimand, tolerance for risk, the value placed on novelty, and the level of freedom members have to act independently (Lipshitz et al., 2002). Cultural norms that constrain individuals' roles within the group or make it difficult to spread knowledge gained by individuals to the rest of the group can hinder group efforts to learn (Romme and Dillen, 1997).[29] Two factors in particular contribute to a pro-learning culture within organizations: group leadership that is positive toward learning and group tolerance for risk.

The words and actions of a group's leaders define the value structure and culture of the group. The commitment of group leaders to learning activities—including how they reward individuals for participating in learning activities, whether they devote resources to innovative efforts, how they react to failed attempts at innovation, and whether they themselves encourage the group to adopt new tactics and op-

---

[26] Emphasizing its commitment to specific types of learning activities, LTTE has reportedly invested up to 40 percent of its war budget in intelligence gathering (Gunaratna, 2001a).

[27] Well-described counterexamples are somewhat elusive, given the lesser incentive to devote detailed analytical attention to lower-profile or apparently less-threatening terrorist groups. Such groups were also not included in our case studies. Examples of organizations that do not devote significant resources to tactical and operational learning—and, as a result, pose threats of a significantly different nature—include racially motivated radical groups whose violent activities are frequently opportunistic (see, for example, Kaplan, 1995; Willems, 1995).

[28] This failure was addressed in the section on absorptive capacity.

[29] Because of the focus on learning in our case studies, we did not examine terrorist groups whose culture was significantly negative toward learning.

tions—determines the group culture with respect to learning.[30] Groups whose leaders do not support learning will be less likely to innovate successfully.

The effect of the leadership on the learning culture of a group is not necessarily uniform across a terrorist organization: Differences among PIRA units, some having leadership that promoted innovation and some having leadership that did not, contributed to some units being better at learning than others (Harnden, 2000; O'Callaghan, 1999, pp. 71, 101–102). Leaders who promote learning value their group members learning from past activities, whether those activities succeeded or failed.[31,32] As noted earlier, PIRA (Collins and McGovern, 1998; O'Doherty, 1993) and JI (International Crisis Group, 2003, p. 17) both used "after-action" reviews of activities and operations to learn from past experience and improve over time. The decision on the part of the groups' leadership to carry out such processes reinforces the value the group places on learning and encourages members to pursue it.

Whether a terrorist group can learn effectively also depends on how tolerant it is of risk. If a group's leadership is willing to accept failed attempts at innovation, members will be more likely to continue to experiment and explore new tactics and technologies. PIRA exemplifies this sort of permissive environment: Even when units' experiments were damaging to the group, the central leadership was reportedly more likely to justify the actions than to punish the individuals involved (Drake, 1998, p. 29). While this could have undermined the group's overall strategic progress, it preserved a culture where individuals were willing to try new things that were potentially useful. In contrast, the members of a terrorist group that is risk averse and punishes individuals when experiments fail will be much less likely to try new things in the future.

To the extent possible, an analyst should bring any available information about a terrorist group's culture to bear in assessing ongoing learning efforts. In groups where innovation is rewarded and supported by group leaders, individuals are more likely to take the risks needed to try new things and more likely to innovate successfully. In contrast, groups with a conservative approach to change or a culture that is unforgiving of failure are less likely to learn successfully.

---

[30] It should be noted that the relevant leadership with respect to terrorist group learning activities may or may not be the same as the political or hierarchical leadership of the group. For example, key members of the "learning leadership" might include technical people within specialized units who might be at least as important as the command structure for influencing group culture for learning.

[31] The Tamil Tigers are an example of a terrorist group whose leadership strongly values learning and therefore encourages it (Gunaratna, 1997).

[32] In contrast, leaders focused on maintaining an appearance of success may be unwilling to examine or even discuss past actions that were not viewed as successful.

Identifying the Knowledge Required for a Group to Learn Successfully

> "Learning will be successful only if the group can bring together the right combination of knowledge to accomplish its goals."

Adopting a new tactic or weapon successfully almost always requires that a terrorist group acquire both explicit and tacit knowledge. Learning will be successful only if the group can bring together the right combination of knowledge to accomplish its goals. Assessment of whether a terrorist group's learning efforts will be successful therefore requires, first, articulation of what the group is trying to do and then identification of the particular combinations of explicit and tacit knowledge needed to do it successfully.[33] After identifying the different routes a group could pursue, the analyst must determine whether it is learning in a way that will enable it to achieve the required knowledge. The necessary combination of tacit and explicit knowledge could either come from outside sources or be developed internally through research and experimentation.

The example of Hizballah is instructive in this regard. In the late 1990s, the group's state sponsors provided it with sophisticated wire-guided TOW antitank missiles (such technologies are a form of explicit knowledge). But those sponsors were unable to give the group the tacit knowledge needed to use the weapons successfully. Because the militaries of Iran and Syria used the weapons in ways that were inappropriate to Hizballah's circumstances, the training they provided was not helpful. The training was based on traditional military doctrine, which included firing the weapons from relatively open positions. This approach is appropriate for large units that can defend themselves against counterattacks, but it was not workable for the small Hizballah units, which could be quickly destroyed in counterattacks. Consequently, the terrorist group had to developing tacit knowledge internally to utilize the weapons in ways that were consistent with its circumstances (Susser, 2000). The group learned to fire the weapons from inside villages and was then able to use them effectively while minimizing the risk to the firing teams.

Because of its leaderless resistance model, the ELF/ALF could be significantly constrained if carrying out its attacks required extensive tacit knowledge. Similarly, if new ELF/ALF "members" (many of whom lack experience in violent activities) have to undertake an extensive learning process, they might be discouraged from acting to advance the movement's agenda. Therefore, ELF/ALF has chosen tactics that require

---

[33] For any given activity, there will likely be more than one combination of essential tacit and explicit knowledge. For example, to carry out sniper operations, a terrorist group could obtain appropriate equipment and training on the international arms market, could build the equipment from scratch and teach its members how to use it, or could select one of a number of other possible acquisition and learning strategies. See, for example, Smithson, 1999, pp. 11–69, for an analysis of the knowledge and expertise required for the acquisition and use of particular types of unconventional weapons.

very little tacit knowledge. The attacks described in ELF/ALF manuals (explicit knowledge disseminated via the Internet) are basic in nature—vandalism, arson, and other simple tactics—and require minimal tacit knowledge to be used successfully (Trujillo, 2005). ELF/ALF has increased the chance that its learning efforts will be successful by constraining those efforts to comparatively modest goals.

Aum's goals presented a much higher hurdle. The successful manufacture of biological weapons requires significant amounts of both tacit and explicit knowledge, including the biology knowledge needed to identify and obtain hazardous organisms, the biochemistry expertise needed to grow them, and multidisciplinary knowledge needed to weaponize and disseminate them efficiently. In its efforts to produce these weapons, Aum Shinrikyo gained part of the required knowledge, but not all, and as a result, its biological weapons program was largely a failure. Although it collected a wide range of relevant explicit knowledge (e.g., published scientific literature), Aum did not seek out relevant sources of tacit knowledge, apparently intent on learning what it needed to learn on its own. This is somewhat surprising, since the group's extensive connections in Russia could have connected it with weapons scientists possessing significant knowledge of these topics (Parachini, 2005). Access to such knowledge sources could have significantly increased the group's ability to produce effective biological agents.

Acting More Effectively to Thwart Terrorist Efforts

Because learning capabilities are highly important for the adaptability and functioning of terrorist organizations, an understanding of how such groups learn could significantly enhance law enforcement and intelligence operations. Knowledge of group learning processes could contribute to evaluating and improving efforts to combat terrorism, and in addition, to the extent that a terrorist group's internal learning processes can be understood, it could suggest novel ways to take on terrorist groups, e.g., by blunting the effectiveness of their learning abilities or using those capabilities against them to undermine their operational effectiveness. As illustrated in Figure 4.5, an understanding of group learning can

- Illuminate the reciprocal relationships between actions to combat terrorism and terrorist group learning efforts
- Suggest novel strategies to combat terrorism that (1) target group learning activities or (2) divert those activities or shape their outcomes

Figure 4.5
Understanding Group Learning to Aid in Action

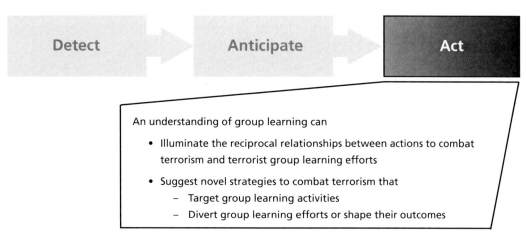

RAND *MG331-4.5*

The Reciprocal Relationship Between Actions to Combat Terrorism and Terrorist Groups' Efforts to Adapt and Change

> "Law enforcement and intelligence planners need to understand how the 'moves' made by security forces shape or determine the 'moves' made by terrorist group adversaries."

Terrorist groups are almost always struggling against a range of security and law enforcement organizations. The actions of those counterterrorist organizations have a direct and powerful effect on what and how terrorist groups learn. Actions taken to combat terrorism provide a powerful incentive for a group to continue to learn, since a terrorist group that does not adapt in response to new security or intelligence measures will, at the minimum, be rendered ineffective or, more likely, will be infiltrated and dismantled. The constant evolution in countermeasures requires terrorist groups to continually move forward simply to preserve their current level of capabilities, a state that has been described as "the technology treadmill" (Hoffman, 1998, p. 180).

In a dynamic contest between organizations,[34] an advantage gained by one side prompts the other side to attempt to offset or degrade that advantage. Law enforcement and intelligence planners need to understand how the "moves" made by security forces shape or determine the "moves" made by terrorist group adversaries.[35] Our

---

[34] For discussion of terrorist groups not included in our case studies, see Cragin and Daly, 2004.

[35] This knowledge could contribute to efforts to understand terrorist organizations as complete systems that can be influenced through a range of mechanisms (Davis and Jenkins, 2002), and also to modeling the give-and-take,

case study groups made a variety of changes to their organizational structures, tactics, and activities in response to security or other pressures. They aimed their activities both at directly countering protective measures and at circumventing the ways law enforcement and intelligence organizations gather the information they need to disrupt attacks and prosecute suspected terrorists.

The terrorist groups also demonstrated their ability to learn directly from security forces, a learning activity that is particularly important when the groups target members of those organizations.[36] PIRA and Hizballah staged a significant fraction of their operations against security forces and military organizations. These terrorist groups exploited opportunities to learn from their opponents, both through observation and by building dedicated intelligence-gathering capabilities. These efforts informed the groups' overall security efforts and helped them to design specific attack operations. Using information it collected on the Israeli military, for example, Hizballah modified its tactics to defeat the military's likely countermoves. Similarly, in designing its attack on a military patrol at Warrenpoint in 1979, PIRA drew on observations of how the British Army had responded in similar incidents at that site (Harnden, 2000, p. 199).

Adaptations by terrorist groups can affect learning efforts carried out by law enforcement, intelligence, or other security force organizations as well. Modifications that terrorist groups make in their operations can render indicators used by intelligence and law enforcement to track and gauge the terrorists' activities (e.g., estimates of a group's weapons stocks) "obsolete." As PIRA became more adept at producing bombs, mortars, and RPGs, it had no need to stockpile these weapons. Instead, it could manufacture a weapon immediately before an attack (Jackson, 2005). This had significant logistical benefits for the group, and it also meant that estimates of stored weapons became a much less valid indicator of the group's capabilities and intent.

Because terrorist groups will always seek to circumvent or defeat measures intended to combat terrorism, this type of back-and-forth learning between the two sides will occur in all such conflicts. To the extent that a deeper understanding of a group's learning processes can enable analysts to anticipate its ability to respond to a given countermeasure, it will be possible to design more-effective interdiction and security measures.

---

measure-countermeasure interactions using game-theory approaches (e.g., Overgaard, 1994; Pate-Cornell and Guikema, 2002; Sandler and Arce M., 2003).

[36] This type of learning can be particularly advantageous against opponents that themselves do not learn or adapt well in response to the terrorists' actions.

Devising New Strategies for Combating Terrorism by Curtailing Group Learning Ability

> "It could be possible to design countermeasures that directly address or even take advantage of the attempts groups make to learn."

Given the potential impact of effective learning, law enforcement and intelligence organizations might seek to reduce the ability of terrorist groups to learn or might attempt to short-circuit their ongoing learning efforts. Yet efforts to combat terrorism frequently do not explicitly address terrorist group learning. Because learning is a route the terrorist organization takes to blunt or circumvent countermeasures, many efforts to combat terrorism only seek to overwhelm the group's ability to learn its way around the counterefforts.

With a sufficiently detailed understanding of terrorist groups' learning processes, it could be possible to design countermeasures that directly address or even take advantage of the attempts groups make to learn.[37] Participants in our project workshop discussions were particularly enthusiastic about the potential contribution of analysis focused on organizational learning to the development of new strategies for combating terrorism. Drawing on those discussions and the results of the case studies, we identified two overarching approaches (Figure 4.6):[38]

- Target group learning activities directly to reduce terrorists' ability to adapt over time
- Take action to divert terrorist groups' learning efforts or influence the outcomes of such efforts

Directly Targeting Terrorist Group Learning Activities

> "This strategy provides an additional potential target to act against: a group's learning system."

Preventing a terrorist group from learning could provide a means of limiting its capabilities overall, even when taking on the group directly might not be possible. An understanding of terrorist group learning efforts could also provide a "force multiplier" effect for traditional efforts to combat terrorism; that is, if such efforts are designed to be as disruptive to group learning processes as possible,

---

[37] Such a strategy is consistent with strategic principles advanced in Thomas and Casebeer, 2004, pp. 70–81.

[38] These approaches are intended to highlight ways in which an understanding of learning could be uniquely useful for planning efforts to combat terrorism. They do not necessarily constitute a comprehensive listing of all the possible learning-directed approaches that are relevant in fighting terrorism. The two approaches should be viewed as promising avenues rather than as definitive proofs of any one avenue's specific value. Focused study will clearly be required to assess the utility and practicality of the routes that appear most promising.

Figure 4.6
Learning-Focused Strategies for Combating Terrorism

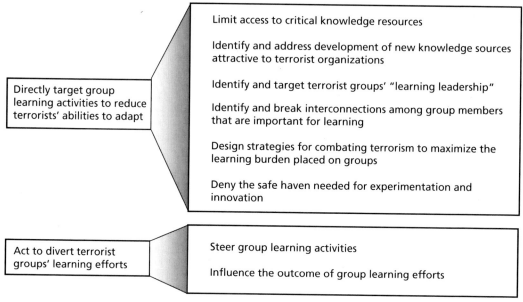

Directly target group learning activities to reduce terrorists' abilities to adapt

Limit access to critical knowledge resources

Identify and address development of new knowledge sources attractive to terrorist organizations

Identify and target terrorist groups' "learning leadership"

Identify and break interconnections among group members that are important for learning

Design strategies for combating terrorism to maximize the learning burden placed on groups

Deny the safe haven needed for experimentation and innovation

Act to divert terrorist groups' learning efforts

Steer group learning activities

Influence the outcome of group learning efforts

RAND *MG331-4.6*

they could provide a boost to a broader effort to damage a group's capability to cause harm. This strategy therefore provides an additional potential target to act against: a terrorist group's "learning system."[39,40] An understanding of group learning processes could help to identify potential vulnerabilities and strategies to exploit them. The following sections describe six potential strategies aimed at undermining a terrorist group's ability to learn and adapt.

Limit Access to Critical Knowledge Resources. Many established efforts to combat terrorism are aimed at restricting the access of terrorist groups to necessary knowledge resources. Programs to control trafficking in weapons, reduce the availability of specific technologies or information, and safeguard nuclear material and other substances of concern are all intended to impact terrorist group learning activities. In addition to such traditional efforts, attempts could be made to undermine group learning processes by either making knowledge resources less attractive to the groups or casting doubt on their trustworthiness. It was normal for the case study groups to consult with outside experts and other knowledge sources to collect infor-

---

[39] Depending on circumstances, key elements of a terrorist group's learning processes may be very difficult to reconstitute after security force intervention damages or destroys them. As a result, those elements may represent particularly attractive targets for action (workshop discussions).

[40] This is consistent with the approach of viewing terrorist organizations as complex systems of different people, functions, and capabilities (Davis and Jenkins, 2002), each of which might be influenced in different ways.

mation and knowledge. Strategies such as well-publicized sting operations that increase the apparent risk of such interactions or attempts to "pollute" knowledge resources[41] could impact learning in some groups.[42]

Information on terrorist group learning could also contribute to better design of programs aimed at denying critical knowledge and better allocating resources among such programs. Understanding the nature of the knowledge required for certain activities and the routes terrorist groups follow to gain that knowledge is important for any effort to limit access to particular types of knowledge. Certain kinds of explicit knowledge can be transferred so readily and widely that any attempt to block that transfer will be ineffectual.[43] Depending on the types of knowledge and expertise held by terrorist groups, other strategies may also have very limited potential benefits. For example, if a group has the capability to manufacture its own weapons, efforts to restrict its access to the arms market will have a much lower payoff than will such efforts against groups that cannot manufacture their own weapons. Since tacit knowledge is much more difficult to transfer, focusing efforts on preventing access to key tacit-knowledge resources may be particularly attractive.[44]

Identify and Address Development of New Knowledge Sources That Are Attractive to Terrorist Organizations. An understanding of terrorist group learning practices can also assist in identifying the development of new knowledge sources that could be particularly useful to terrorist groups and could inform efforts to prevent terrorists from gaining access to such sources. Arms manufacturers are moving toward systems that require considerably less tacit knowledge to be used effectively. For example, advanced infantry weapons are currently being developed that capture, in both hardware and software, much of the knowledge that would be needed to use them successfully for specialized functions. For older generations of precision firearms, such as sniper rifles,[45] soldiers had to accrue significant amounts of tacit knowledge on such topics as range estimation and correction for environmental in-

---

[41] For example, countering Internet information on bomb making with seemingly authentic but ineffective recipes.

[42] In all cases, the potential benefit of such strategies (which would depend heavily on the specific terrorist group being targeted) would have to be weighed against their inherent uncertainty and potential negative consequences.

[43] For example, the transmission of basic data on tactics and their success through the media (for example, Holden's 1986 analysis of the contagiousness of airline hijackings) or widely reported general vulnerability information.

[44] Established efforts to discourage weapons scientists from collaborating with terrorist organizations provide an excellent example. Depending on the context, targeted initiatives might be designed to discourage individuals with specific military knowledge, "insider data" on key infrastructures or other targets, or other relevant tacit knowledge from interacting with or otherwise instructing terrorist organizations.

[45] For example, the Barrett 90 and Belgian FN sniper rifles used by PIRA in attacks on security forces (Harnden, 2000).

fluences.[46] The new weapons incorporate technology systems that carry out these functions, eliminating much of the learning requirement (Cutshaw, 2002). Such advances significantly "lower the bar" in terms of learning for terrorist organizations. If analogous technologies had been available at the time, PIRA would have avoided the significant difficulties it encountered with RPGs, since the tacit knowledge would have been built into the weapons themselves (Jackson, 2005). As advanced technologies are developed, incorporating measures that limit the ability of unauthorized persons to use the weapons or reduce the chances of their falling into terrorists' hands becomes much more important.[47]

Identify and Target Terrorist Groups' "Learning Leadership." Knowledge of a terrorist group's learning processes could also be used to better target key individuals and thereby limit a group's ability to adapt and evolve. Identification of key individuals is a frequent element of efforts to combat terrorism (see, e.g., Kenney, 2003a). By focusing on how a group learns, analysts may be able to identify individual members who play key roles in learning processes. In some terrorist groups, leaders play a central role in group interpretation efforts and represent key vulnerabilities. One such individual was Aum's Asahara (Parachini, 2005). While the capture of central individuals could clearly have a broad effect on group learning capabilities, a terrorist group's "learning leadership" may or may not be the same as its political or organizational leadership. The learning leaders could be technical specialists or individuals who play important roles in managing or supporting the learning efforts of others in the group.[48]

Identify and Break Interconnections Among Terrorist Group Members That Are Important for Learning. Past studies of social networks within terrorist groups have produced a range of insights into how the interconnections among individual members of groups or among subunits of a larger organization affect group functioning and performance (see, for example, Carley et al., 2001). These studies map information such as communications traffic, meetings, family connections, or shared experiences among individuals to discern the nature of the networks that exist inside organizations. They have suggested that because of the importance of interpersonal

---

[46] This is in stark contrast to general-purpose assault weapons, such as the AK-47 and Armalite rifle, which (when used for nonspecialized functions) require a minimal amount of expertise/tacit knowledge to be used effectively: "The virtue [of the Armalite] is that it is easy to use. It must be stressed again that most urban guerrillas learn on the job. Very few have fired many shots in practice. Very few have had any formal military training. Very few handle weapons with special skill. The Armalite, in particular, does not need very special skills" (Bell, 1987, p. 53).

[47] Of course, such newer, more-sophisticated weapons also are far more expensive and may require specialized maintenance practices. While lowering the bar in one regard, they may raise it in another.

[48] Steven and Gunaratna cite Israeli targeting of Yahiya Ayyash, "the Engineer," a key bombmaker in Hamas, as an example of this tactic. However, the response to the action is also instructive: The terrorist group began to train and disperse larger numbers of bombmakers to limit the chance of their capabilities being similarly damaged again (Steven and Gunaratna, 2004, pp. 185–186).

connections to a terrorist group's ability to act, targeting the linkages among the members of an organization would be an attractive way to degrade its cohesion and capability. Successfully targeting key nodes in a terrorist group's network could prevent coordination among different parts of the organization or could even cause the group to fall apart.

An understanding of terrorist group learning activities would provide an additional element to such analyses. To the extent that group learning processes are understood and members are known to investigators, those who play key roles in group learning processes could be targeted.[49] Individuals who are key for group learning may or may not be the same as those identified using other social-network-related variables such as communications traffic. Information about the effectiveness of a terrorist group's internal network—for example, whether it is effective at transferring tacit as well as explicit knowledge—could enhance such analyses to enable better targeting of disruptive efforts.

Although breaking up terrorist group interconnections is promising, caution should be used in designing and implementing such an approach. The effects of such an intervention could be quite different in different groups. Those whose learning efforts rely on direction and coordination through centralized nodes may be unable to recover if those nodes are eliminated. However, breaking individual units away from their larger group could also free those units from learning constraints imposed by the overall organization. The differences observed in innovative activities among PIRA's units, for example, suggest that the additional individual unit autonomy such interventions could produce might generate *more* variety and experimentation at the tactical level than would exist if centralized control was maintained (Jackson, 2005). To the extent that a terrorist group's reaction to such operations could be anticipated on the basis of its past history, the potential costs and benefits of these types of interventions could be more clearly assessed.

Design Strategies to Maximize the Learning Burden Placed on Groups. An understanding of how specific terrorist groups learn may make it possible to design measures that maximize the burden placed on group learning and minimize the groups' ability to respond through adaptive behavior (workshop discussions). Such "counteradaptive strategies" (see Gerwehr and Glenn, 2003, pp. 49–57, where this concept is introduced) would seek to maximize the disruptive effects of such measures. Examples of counteradaptive strategies include (Gerwehr and Glenn, 2003; workshop discussions)

- **Using combinations of different approaches.** A group has some maximum number of different learning tasks that it can carry out simultaneously. If multi-

---

[49] Steven and Gunaratna (2004) describe such actions as targeting the "middle management" of terrorist organizations.

ple counterterrorism measures are applied at once, a group may not have sufficient learning capability to respond effectively to all of them.[50]

- **Building randomness into the application of counterterrorism strategies.** A key part of all learning processes is discerning cause-and-effect relationships between a group's actions and the outcomes they produce. A reasonable level of randomness in the way different counterterrorism techniques are applied—for example, randomness in intensity, time, and nature—could limit terrorist groups' ability to assess the counterterrorist efforts and build response strategies.

- **Adjusting the timing and speed of the application of countermeasures.** No matter how great its capabilities, a terrorist group needs time to carry out learning activities and implement their results. Adjusting the timing of counterterrorism actions—for example, by introducing new measures in rapid succession or quickly shifting tactics from one type of counterstrategy to a very different one—could limit a group's ability to learn and respond effectively.

The specific requirements for developing and implementing counteradaptive strategies will differ among terrorist organizations. Building an understanding of a group's learning behaviors, including the limits of its learning capabilities, is a critical starting point for making such strategies available to law enforcement and intelligence planners.

Deny the Safe Haven Needed for Experimentation and Innovation. Another well-established strategy for combating terrorism is denial of sanctuaries or safe havens. While safe havens are useful to organizations for many reasons, they are particularly important for research, experimentation, training, and other learning-related activities. PIRA, JI, Hizballah, and Aum all utilized different types of safe havens to carry out their learning activities. Similarly, the availability of safe havens was related to terrorist groups' willingness to set up and use more-effective information storage systems such as computer archives and physical records.[51,52]

To deny terrorist groups safe havens as effectively as possible, law enforcement and intelligence planners must be able to define what constitutes a safe haven for specific group activities. For example, the level of sanctuary a terrorist group requires for basic experimentation with explosive devices is very different from that required for a large-scale military training program. Knowledge of the learning requirements for specific activities of concern would facilitate analysis of what might be the minimal

---

[50] The specific combination of measures and the number of different measures that would need to be combined to overwhelm a terrorist group's learning capability probably differ considerably from group to group.

[51] Anthony Davis (2002) describes a set of al Qaeda's computerized files, including personnel data on individual group members, seized in Afghanistan.

[52] Invading safe havens to destroy such storage systems has been highlighted by others as a key counterterrorism mission (Simmons et al., 2003).

requirements for a corresponding safe haven. Such an analysis could help ensure that actions to eliminate havens have the desired effect (workshop discussions).

Intervening to Divert Terrorist Group Learning or Shape Its Outcomes

> "Law enforcement and intelligence agencies could potentially attempt to directly affect the nature and outcome of terrorist group learning activities."

Rather than attempting to directly prevent a terrorist group from learning, strategies could also be designed to take a less direct approach. *Diverting* group learning efforts is a fundamental goal of most efforts to combat terrorism. If a group is concerned about its own security and the potential for infiltration by intelligence or law enforcement operatives, it will be forced to focus learning resources on defensive measures rather than offensive operations.[53] As a result, even the most generic counterefforts can provide the opportunity to shift a terrorist group's "learning budget" in ways that could reduce the outward threat the group poses. A more direct approach to influencing terrorist group learning can be found in stated policies of massive retaliation against terrorist groups that use certain types of weapons. Such policies, generally aimed at the use of unconventional weapons, seek to deter terrorist groups from undertaking the learning needed to acquire those weapons in the first place (see, for example, Jenkins, 2002).[54]

Beyond these strategies for general deterrence and influencing group learning decisions, law enforcement and intelligence agencies could potentially attempt to directly affect the nature and outcome of terrorist group learning activities. If a sufficiently detailed model of a group's learning processes and capabilities were available, use of deception,[55] misinformation,[56] and other psychological operations could make it possible to

---

[53] This effect is discussed by Moghadam with reference to Palestinian groups (Moghadam, 2003).

[54] Terrorist group concerns about security at desired targets, technical countermeasures, and other steps that increase operational uncertainty can also affect the way groups allocate learning resources. Such measures can induce groups to devote more time and effort to planning individual operations—to increase their "robustness" against the countermeasures and increase their chance of success—and therefore might constrain the total number of separate operations a group is able to carry out.

[55] Significant work has been performed on the theory and practical implementation of deception operations, both in a traditional military context and in the targeting of nonstate actors such as terrorist groups (see, for example, Gerwehr and Glenn, 2000, 2003). We do not attempt to address this literature in any comprehensive way; rather, we are simply highlighting the relevance of the technique to influencing terrorist group learning.

[56] Workshop participants also pointed out that such operations could provide a way to gather primary information on terrorist group learning processes. After specific types of information are released to known representatives of an organization, the "progress" of the information through group distribution channels can be monitored as a way of mapping out information flows or their effect on terrorist group behavior to provide insights into the group's interpretation process (workshop discussions).

- Steer terrorist group learning in particular directions
- Influence the results of terrorist groups' learning efforts[57]

Steer Terrorist Group Learning Activities. Deception and other influence techniques could be aimed at steering a terrorist group away from specific learning activities that could increase the threat it poses. Influence operations could seek to guide groups toward technologies that are more readily traced, operations that are less damaging or easier to thwart, or other organizationally dysfunctional paths. Such operations could also be aimed at degrading specific components of a terrorist group's learning processes. For example, given the potential benefits of sophisticated organizational memories to group learning capabilities, operations could attempt to increase terrorist groups' perceptions of the risk of building tangible memory resources.[58] These operations could be as basic as publicizing key seizures of information from group memories such as computer systems or files; misinformation could be used if no actual seizures had taken place.[59]

Influence the Outcome of Terrorist Group Learning Processes. Research on organizational learning presents a range of other potential targets for deception and influence operations. Because of the complexity of the environment faced by most organizations, it is often difficult for even the best strategic planner to determine with certainty whether the choices he or she is making really help achieve the organization's goals. Researchers call this "causal ambiguity" (Lipshitz et al., 2002; Zollo and Winter, 2002; Taudes et al., 2002, and references therein)—a difficulty in correctly linking something that has happened to an organization, whether good or bad, to its appropriate cause.[60] Similarly, many organizations are afflicted by predispositions in the types of information they seek and the rules they apply to interpret the information. Researchers have particularly highlighted these types of problems in terrorist

---

[57] Carrying out such influence operations with any degree of certainty of effectiveness would require a high level of information on a target group's learning activities. Depending on the practical realities of operations against specific terrorist groups, an agency might be positioned to act more directly against an adversary group before it could capture sufficient information to carry out these types of operations with any degree of certainty. Nevertheless, influence operations could provide a complementary option even without complete information, assuming that the costs of the operations were commensurate with the more uncertain payoff.

[58] Terrorist groups' learning processes can themselves be the subject of learning; that is, terrorist organizations can seek to "learn to learn better." In this case, the goal of the influence operation would be to thwart that process and lead the group to conclusions that result in less learning capability.

[59] Carrying out deception and influence operations against a terrorist organization would require significant information on the mechanisms through which the terrorist group gathers information and interprets that information. Workshop participants viewed the reliance of the case study groups on a wide variety of knowledge sources as potentially useful from a deception standpoint, as it provides a variety of ways to inject information into a group's deliberative processes.

[60] This can be even more of a problem for groups without centralized control, as individual parts of the group may be changing many things simultaneously in an effort to improve performance. Even if performance does improve, it is difficult to determine what change was responsible.

groups, whose clandestine nature and high level of threat can skew behavior and decisionmaking (for example, Bell, 1994, p. 127; McCauley, 2002).

Under certain circumstances, deception and influence operations could try to capitalize on these "natural" failures in terrorist group learning. For example, deceiving a group about the impact of its operations could make ineffective tactics appear more attractive or make successful techniques appear to fail (workshop discussions).[61] Injecting a level of random disinformation into terrorist groups' data streams could similarly seek to maximize ambiguities about the effectiveness of particular operations.[62] In all cases, the goal of influence operations would be to alter the terrorist group's perception of its efforts and of the costs and benefits of its current behaviors or potential future operational options.

---

[61] Such deception regarding this type of "damage assessment" would obviously be inappropriate in most cases, given the wide dissemination of information about most terrorist events.

[62] These types of comparatively sophisticated operations would likely require detailed information on terrorist groups' learning efforts and their interpretation processes in particular. For example, operations planners would need to know whether group decisionmakers relied on single sources of information or based decisions on a broader array of evidence, how they weighted different types of information, how they judged success and failure, and how the terrorist group was likely to react as a result: Will the group "give up" after one failure or will it focus on learning from the failure as it designs a subsequent attempt? If it chooses to learn from the failure, the potential benefits of this type of operation would be significantly reduced. In the absence of these data, the chance of such operations being successful would be considerably reduced and could risk sending "the wrong message," producing unintended and unpredictable results.

CHAPTER FIVE

Limitations of an Organizational-Learning-Based Approach for Analysis and Operational Planning in Combating Terrorism

On the basis of our analysis and discussions with law enforcement and intelligence professionals, we believe that an organizational-learning-based approach to analyzing terrorist group behavior can make significant contributions to planning and operations for combating terrorism. However, this approach would not necessarily be appropriate in every situation.

The Need to Understand Terrorist Group Structure and Membership

An organizational-learning-based framework can be useful for understanding terrorist group activities and behaviors only if information is available about the organization[1] involved. Because learning activities and processes go on inside an organization, the analyst must have enough information on these internal workings to build a plausible model of the organization—a model that provides a starting point for framing and testing hypotheses about the group's learning behaviors. For example, if a terrorist organization's membership is completely unknown, it is very difficult to frame questions and test hypotheses about how information is distributed among its members and how that distribution could affect the group's ability to learn.[2] Building models based on available intelligence data is a central task for any analyst studying terrorist

---

[1] It is also relevant to note that an analytical approach focused on organizational learning is useful only for describing the actions of groups. Such concepts as "distribution of knowledge" and "organizational memory" are not applicable to terrorist activities carried out by individuals in isolation. Individuals must still learn what they need to know to carry out their violent activities, but organizational learning concepts are not appropriate for understanding that process. The learning challenges faced by individual terrorists due to their lack of organization have been cited as an argument why such "amateur terrorism" poses an overall lower threat level (Tucker, 2001, p. 135).

[2] The lack of models for terrorist "fronts" or "movements" that use a leaderless resistance strategy (such as ELF/ALF) makes application of such frameworks problematic.

group behavior.[3] As a result, although the requirement for detailed information on internal group processes may limit the applicability of these approaches, it is less of a barrier than might be initially assumed, and it can be directly addressed by intelligence and law enforcement in the design of collection priorities.

Analysts of group learning activities must also carefully select the most appropriate "unit of analysis" for a terrorist group's learning activities. In some terrorist organizations, the entire group may be involved in learning. In others, only subunits of the group may be actively learning. Aum Shinrikyo's biological and chemical weapons research was carried out by a small group of people close to Asahara, the group's leader. Viewing the entire cult, which had tens of thousands of members, as the unit of analysis would therefore not be appropriate and would lead to invalid conclusions (Parachini, 2005). Similarly, within PIRA, different units learned with very different degrees of effectiveness; the elite units reportedly carried out the most-advanced learning activities (Jackson, 2005). Modeling the learning activities of ELF/ALF is even more complex, since the lack of strong connections among even its smallest subunits means that the organization cannot learn in the same way that more closely connected and coordinated groups do (Trujillo, 2005). The literature does not provide an unambiguous definition of "organization" for the purposes of studying organizational learning. Rather, it highlights the importance of considering—and collecting—the necessary information to determine whether an entire organization is involved in learning or learning varies among subunits of the group.

Lack of Data on Terrorist Group Learning Processes

To understand organizational learning in any group, it is necessary to have information on the processes the group uses to gather knowledge, to interpret it, to distribute it, and to store it in an organizational memory. Such data are often difficult to collect. Even for organizations that are open to study, analysts must frequently rely on survey or other techniques to collect relevant information from individual group members. Data on an organization's outputs, which can indicate learning-induced change, are also frequently difficult to collect because of the inability to identify and measure all the different outputs.

These problems are multiplied for terrorist groups. Though significant data are frequently available on terrorist incidents where groups act overtly, data on other actions may be difficult to obtain. Information on failed operations by organizations

---

[3] Examination of a terrorist group's learning behavior can provide an opportunity to test and validate currently accepted models of the group's structure and internal activities. Data on its knowledge-gathering activities, loci of interpretation, likely distribution pathways and modes, and sites of organizational memory can also be used to critique the model. For example, learning activities that appear inconsistent with the assumed group structure may help to identify problems in a model.

that have effective internal operational security practices may not be available. In addition, the validity of data used to evaluate terrorist groups' activities and prowess may be damaged by reporting biases or the actions of others, such as clandestine disruption of terrorist operations unknown to the analyst examining apparent failures. Depending on the nature of ongoing operations against a terrorist organization, the impact of law enforcement or intelligence operations, both U.S. and particularly those of other nations, could significantly bias available data on group activities. Such complications make it more difficult to apply learning-focused models to specific groups, but this limitation is also within the control of intelligence and law enforcement organizations via the design of focused information-gathering efforts.

The Nature of Learning Models

An analysis built on an understanding of terrorist organizational learning behavior addresses changes in group activities over time. Learning-based theories focus on understanding individual terrorist attacks, activities, or behaviors as part of an overall pattern within a history of previous actions. They cannot provide insight into individual terrorist events in isolation. In the context of operational histories, the implications of learning activities could be quite different for different terrorist organizations. For example, the concepts of continuous and discontinuous learning are relative: A change that might be an incremental part of a process of continuous improvement for one terrorist group might represent a major change in another. Building a new type of weapon could be an incremental change for a group that was experienced in machining weapons; adopting the same weapon would be a much more drastic shift for a group without that experience. Consequently, an analysis built on an understanding of how a terrorist group learns needs to address changes in a group's activities over time. For instance, information on changes can help to assess whether a given terrorist event is consistent with or is a significant departure from a group's past learning history. It could also assist in evaluating whether a specific threat is credible: The further a threat diverges from the terrorist group's past efforts and the more extreme the learning requirements for carrying it out successfully are, the less credible it is.

Difficulties in Measuring the Results of Learning

Throughout this report, we have largely assumed that law enforcement or intelligence analysts could readily recognize and unambiguously measure the effects of terrorist group learning. However, while the general concept of learning is easy to articulate, it is much more difficult to understand fully and measure all of the changes that result from learning in an organization.

In general, the result of learning is a change in an organization's "level of knowledge." If, by evaluating its behaviors or pursuing new options or technologies, an organization gains knowledge that could improve its performance—even if it has not yet put that knowledge to use—it has learned. But measuring the *results* of a group's learning process entails gathering data on how its stock of knowledge changed as a result of its learning effort. It is difficult to assess changes in the level of knowledge within an organization because measures of that knowledge are largely inaccessible to the outside analyst.[4]

Measuring learning, therefore, is frequently driven toward *observable* indicators of either an organization's potential for change or the results of its change efforts as a proxy for direct measurement.[5] For incremental change, such indicators include observable changes in the way a group carries out its activities (coupled with any information on the reasons for the changes) and the results of those activities. For discontinuous change, indicators include group discussions about and considerations of new activities or changes and observable shifts in group practices after such changes are implemented. Reliance on observable data risks missing components of learning that do not produce obvious results, but it does capture many relevant outputs.

There is a range of potential observable indicators for both continuous and discontinuous change in terrorist groups. Novelty is a clear signal: When a group adopts a new weapon or uses a new tactic, the shifts in group behavior are most clear. There are also a number of potential observable indicators of continuous improvement in terrorist organizations, including improvements in a group's ability to

- Evade penetration and arrest
- Use its chosen weapons accurately and effectively
- Reliably and reproducibly execute particular operations
- Gather timely and relevant intelligence
- Stage attacks resulting in increasing economic damage
- Increase the numbers of fatalities and injuries per attack

---

[4] For example, Bohn (1994) frames the measurement of learning in terms of the understanding and control a group has over the technologies and techniques it is using. While such an approach is attractive because it directly addresses how consistently and effectively a group can apply those tools, it is difficult to measure the results from outside the group.

[5] The terrorist group itself may also have difficulty in observing the effects of its learning activities. In some areas, group members will be able to get information to assess their activities and guide future efforts—for example, data on the performance of weapons reported by their users or information on how far improvised rockets flew and their accuracy from media reports. In other areas, such as specific details of the performance of explosive devices, most of the "data" will be impossible to collect or interpret because of the violence of the event. In such cases, even the terrorist group itself must base its judgments on the available directly observable information and on theories about why operations evolved or devices performed as they did.

Despite the variety of potential metrics, it is not always immediately clear how to assess changes with respect to terrorist group learning. Not all change is learning; to be considered learning, the change must benefit the organization in its effort to accomplish its goals. As a result, to measure learning, the analyst must be able to measure not just change, but how that change increases the effectiveness of the group's actions or increases their probability of success.[6] This requirement highlights two problems:

- **Difficulty in selecting appropriate indicators for terrorists' tactical-level activities.** Since it is not always clear what a group is trying to accomplish in a given operation, it may not be obvious which indicators are appropriate for comparing a group's "tactical performance" in different operations.[7]
- **Difficulties linking observable indicators to terrorist group strategic progress.** Because it is difficult to draw a clear link between terrorists' activities at the tactical level—i.e., individual operations—and progress toward the group's strategic goals (which may be unknown or not completely known), it is often unclear whether or not changes in "tactical performance" help or hurt the group's chances of strategic success.

Difficulties in Selecting Appropriate Indicators for Terrorists' Tactical-Level Activities

To determine whether the results of a particular terrorist attack, from the perspective of the terrorist organization, are better or worse than those of a previous one, the analyst needs some insight into what the group was trying to accomplish. For example, a bombing operation might be intended to result in economic damages, human casualties, or both. Having some picture of the goals of an operation—whether through collecting information directly or by having enough circumstantial data to make an educated guess—is necessary to select the right indicators to describe its results and compare them to previous attacks by the same group. Measuring an attack with the wrong yardstick—e.g., assessing a bombing aimed at causing fatalities as if it were intended to damage economic targets, or vice versa—can result in erroneous conclusions about a group's learning efforts. Individual indicators that are relevant for specific terrorist groups in some circumstances[8] will not be relevant in others.

---

[6] This difficulty has led some researchers away from definitions of learning that include such value judgments and toward definitions that focus only on change or on other measures that are independent of the end result of the changes.

[7] This is further complicated by the fact that a group's tactical goals may shift over time as its strategy evolves. However, changes in performance can help shed light on the terrorist group's goals.

[8] The results of the case studies indicate that such tactical indicators appear easiest to apply to groups engaged in ongoing terrorist-insurgent campaigns, such as PIRA or Hizballah. (See also Moghadam, 2003, p. 79, which discusses similar issues vis-à-vis Palestinian suicide bombings.)

Difficulties Linking Observable Indicators to Terrorist Group Strategic Progress

Although some results of terrorists' tactical activities, such as victims injured and physical or economic damage, are easy to observe, connecting those *results* to the *outcomes* the organization is trying to attain is much less clear. Assessing whether or not change actually benefits an organization's chances of being strategically successful is quite difficult.[9] It is not clear, for example, how a terrorist group gaining a particular new weapon or increasing its level of lethality affects the group's chance of strategic success without the benefit of hindsight after the impact of the changes has played out and been resolved. The same change could be either beneficial or detrimental for different groups. For example, killing more people per attack may be in a terrorist group's long-term strategic interest if its goals can be accomplished by constantly ramping up the fatalities it causes. However, significant increases in fatalities could strategically hurt a group that is trying to maintain a moderate image and maintain a level of legitimacy, e.g., for eventual participation in political negotiations. This makes learning at this higher, strategic level extremely difficult to measure and assess.[10]

Understanding the Contribution of Learning Ability to Specific Terrorist Operations

Understanding how a terrorist group learns is always very useful for estimating how successful the group will be in developing new capabilities or acquiring new tactics. But such understanding is not always as useful for assessing the group's chances of success in specific operations. Depending on the types of targets a terrorist group chooses to attack, significant learning—intelligence gathering, modification of operational plans, or even development of particular weapons—may be needed before an operation can be carried out successfully (Bell, 1998a, p. 262). Groups that select high-profile, well-protected targets because of their visibility or attractiveness from a prestige perspective may have to be particularly good learners. Analytical approaches based on learning can be useful in assessing the activities of these groups and the chance that they will be able to carry out their plans.

In other circumstances, a terrorist group may not need to learn very much to plan an operation and carry it out successfully. If a group focuses on selecting vulnerable targets—sites or individuals it can attack successfully with the weapons and tac-

---

[9] See Merari, 1993, pp. 224–242, for a discussion of levels of strategic success resulting from terrorist violence.

[10] In addition to affecting the ability of the analyst or researcher, such difficulties also affect decisionmakers within the terrorist organizations. The ambiguities in the impact of changes on strategic success therefore hurt groups' ability to interpret their own actions and outcomes as they try to craft strategy and tactics.

tics it has available[11]—there may be few learning requirements.[12] Learning capabilities will be less of a factor determining the success or failure of these attacks.

Analysis can be further complicated by the fact that a single terrorist group may not fall cleanly into one of these two categories. As a group's strategy changes or its focus shifts over time, the way it chooses its targets may change, moving it from one category to the other. Such a behavioral shift was observed in JI. Some of the operations it selected involved high-profile, hardened targets and as a result involved considerable learning; other targets were apparently selected because they were soft and accessible (Baker, 2005). Similarly, different cells within a single terrorist group may have different targeting strategies. Some units within PIRA reportedly selected targets almost entirely based on their vulnerability; in other cases, specialized teams identified high-profile attack opportunities and carried out the full complement of learning processes required to mount the operations (Jackson, 2005).[13] Because of such differences, the analyst using an organizational-learning-based model must understand how the terrorist group's targeting behavior might affect the impact of its learning ability on its chances of operational success, and vice-versa.

---

[11] Note that this qualification does not discount the importance of the terrorist group's learning ability for putting those capabilities in place initially.

[12] Significant learning may be required before a terrorist group develops the skills needed to successfully select such vulnerable, or "soft," targets.

[13] Although not the primary focus of this discussion, the particular targeting strategy a terrorist group adopts and the learning requirements for successfully carrying out that strategy could have a significant impact on target hardening and the design of other countermeasures. For terrorist groups that primarily select targets based on vulnerability to current attack options, comparatively modest security measures—"just enough to bring the target above the group's available capabilities"—should be sufficient to deter attack. For terrorist groups that are willing and able to commit significant learning resources to attacking desirable targets, the targets would have to be hardened beyond the terrorists' ability to overcome the security through learning. This is a much higher threshold for design.

CHAPTER SIX

Conclusions

To protect the public against the threat posed by terrorist organizations, law enforcement and intelligence organizations must

- Assess the threat and understand the behavior of individual terrorist groups
- Develop and implement effective counterstrategies to detect and thwart terrorist groups' efforts
- Appropriately allocate resources against potential and proven adversaries and develop metrics to assess the effectiveness of measures for combating terrorism

Studying how terrorist groups learn can be a valuable addition to the intelligence and law enforcement "tool box" to help in accomplishing all three of these tasks.

Assessing the Threat Posed by Individual Terrorist Groups and Understanding Their Behavior

Examining the behavior of terrorist groups from an organizational learning perspective presents a mixed picture of their successes and failures. Certain groups have shown very significant capacities to learn and innovate, competing effectively with law enforcement and intelligence organizations and building the capabilities needed to carry out complex operations. Others have had difficulty learning effectively and have been limited in their ability to adapt to changing circumstances. Terrorist groups are not uniform in their learning capability, adapting very effectively in some areas, while remaining largely unsuccessful in others. Because learning contributes directly to the threat level of a terrorist group—by determining the tactics it could bring to bear, the weapons it could have available, and the operations it could plan and execute—understanding learning capabilities is a key element of threat assessment.

Modeling the way terrorist groups learn can also provide a way to analyze or project potential changes in their threat level over time. A framework for understanding group learning activities could help inform analysts about a group's efforts to pursue new capabilities, weapons, or tactics. A learning-focused approach could similarly assist in more fully understanding the potential implications on group learning of specific activities, from engaging state sponsors to gaining safe havens for experimentation and training. Projections of how terrorist groups will change in the future based only on the past history of those groups are essentially educated guesses. To the extent that an analyst can truly understand the processes through which a group adapts, those projections can become real forecasts, enabling better planning and policy design for combating terrorism.

Developing and Implementing Effective Counterstrategies

While an understanding of organizational learning in terrorist groups provides no "silver bullet" for addressing the problem of terrorism, it does provide a knowledge base for developing new strategies to target these groups' activities and undermine their capabilities. A deeper understanding of learning can better illuminate the reciprocal relationship between actions to combat terrorism and terrorist groups' learning efforts. Actions aimed at infiltrating and undermining terrorist organizations can have both positive and negative effects on their learning activities. The better possible reactions can be understood, the greater the chance that law enforcement or intelligence actions can be designed to shape those reactions to the public's benefit rather than to the terrorists' advantage.

Organizational-learning-based models can provide alternative approaches to the terrorism problem. Such alternative frameworks and approaches for undermining components of terrorists' activities may be accessible even when more traditional approaches are not. Alternatively, they might play an important complementary or supplemental role, an additional ingredient in a comprehensive, multifront approach to countering terrorist violence.

Allocating Resources and Developing Metrics to Assess the Effectiveness of Efforts to Combat Terrorism

Because the resources available for combating terrorism are finite, decisions must be made about how those resources should be allocated. There will frequently be more worthwhile leads, promising tips, or potential threats than there are resources to pursue them. Allocating resources among all the potential avenues of investigation and among all the possible terrorist groups that could pose a threat to the public and the nation is therefore a critical challenge. The goal is to press hardest on groups that pose the most significant proven or potential threat—groups that do not just have plans and intent, but can readily build the capabilities to carry out those plans. If resources for combating terrorism are arrayed against the wrong groups or devoted to pursuing threats that are not credible, they will be diverted from pursuing more-dangerous terrorist groups.

It is a group's ability to learn that connects what it wants to do with the capability to do it successfully. A terrorist group's ability to adapt and evolve enables it to gather the intelligence needed to stage attacks, to acquire the tactics and weapons necessary for its operations, and to circumvent the security and other countermeasures protecting its desired targets in the dynamic world of countermeasures. An understanding of how terrorist groups learn can, therefore, contribute to decisions about how to allocate available resources for combating terrorism. Organizations that are good learners are potentially more serious threats. For groups acting as parts of international terrorist networks, providing assistance to or cooperating with other terrorist groups, the ability to learn is of serious concern because of what good learners can bring to such interactions as well as what they can gain from them.

Terrorist groups whose efforts are more likely to succeed present a more credible threat and should be a higher priority for law enforcement and intelligence agencies. Groups that can learn effectively may therefore merit special attention and resources, both in an effort to degrade their learning capabilities and because that learning ability may make them particularly difficult targets for counterefforts. To the extent that the law enforcement or intelligence analyst can identify terrorist groups that cannot learn or that learn with more difficulty, other options become available. Groups that do not learn well may be particularly vulnerable—minimal action could permanently remove or reduce the threat they pose, essentially neutralizing them in a way that permits law enforcement and intelligence resources to be allocated to more-pressing threats.

An understanding of terrorist group learning efforts can similarly contribute to the development of better metrics for assessing efforts to combat terrorism. To measure the effectiveness of counterefforts, an analyst must be able to assess the impact of those efforts on terrorist group activities. Reductions in terrorist group capabilities, disruption in operations, limiting groups' ability to successfully stage specific types of attacks, or capture of key assets or individuals could be reasonable components of such metrics. An understanding of terrorist group learning could improve the breadth and accuracy of metrics for assessing efforts to combat terrorism, for example, by contributing to better measures of the effects of counterefforts on groups' capabilities, estimates of how easily groups can learn to defeat the countermeasures, or assessments of the importance of specific captured individuals to groups' learning capability.

Concluding Remarks

This research effort began with two straightforward questions:

- What is known about how terrorist groups learn?
- Can law enforcement and intelligence use knowledge about group learning in their efforts to combat terrorism?

Our analysis of five case study groups and our discussions with law enforcement and intelligence professionals provided answers to both questions, suggesting ways that knowledge about organizational learning can be applied now and also suggesting areas that require more attention to produce the greatest benefits for combating terrorism. It is easiest to address these two questions in reverse order.

The answer to the second question is an emphatic "yes." Because of the importance of organizational learning and the variety of strategies through which knowledge of terrorist group learning could be applied in analysis and operational planning, understanding organizational learning and collecting information about how terrorist groups learn could be very valuable. Our discussions with law enforcement and intelligence professionals indicated that application of a learning-focused approach to analyzing information about terrorist groups and planning operations aimed at thwarting their efforts could provide real benefits.

The answer to the first question is more mixed. Information on the ways even prominent, well-studied terrorist organizations learn is difficult to obtain. Some insights about learning can be extracted from studies that have been carried out for other reasons, but blind spots remain, particularly regarding the most internal components of the process, such as interpretation and decisionmaking activities. Yet these internal components are perhaps of greatest interest to the analyst studying terrorist groups' learning behavior. Information on groups that have garnered less analytical attention would likely be even more difficult to obtain.

Therefore, consistent with the exploratory nature of this project, it is clear that we need to know more. To build a better and broader understanding of organizational learning in terrorist groups, more information is needed—particularly the first-person, internal information available in accounts of former group members or collected from current members when opportunities present themselves. Beyond the need for additional data, our research identified other avenues that should be explored and hypotheses that should be tested in an effort to provide more effective tools for combating terrorism. However, in spite of the need for further investigation, it is our hope that the results presented here can make a contribution to ongoing efforts against terrorist organizations and can assist in developing increasingly effective strategies to protect society from terrorist violence.

Overview of the Case Study Groups

Aum Shinrikyo

Officially registered with the Japanese government as a religious group, Aum Shinrikyo (Supreme Truth) gradually evolved into a terrorist organization that conducted assassinations, ran programs to develop and procure unconventional weapons, plotted to overthrow the Japanese government, and contemplated cataclysmic war with the United States. Aum, founded in 1984 by Shoko Asahara, the organization's charismatic leader and spiritual guru, began as a 15-person yoga and meditation group. Eight years later, it had grown into a movement with nearly 50,000 members, hundreds of millions of dollars in assets, and facilities or activities in Japan, the United States, Germany, Russia, Taiwan, and Sri Lanka. Eventually, the group suffered political defeat and had growing difficulties recruiting and retaining members, after which its rhetoric became increasingly apocalyptic, paranoid, and violent. Asahara claimed that the organization had a divine mission to hasten the apocalypse with the expectation that the only survivors would be the devout followers of Aum. His inner circle of devotees ran the group's programs to acquire weapons of mass destruction, conducted its violent attacks, and, by some accounts, also attempted to cause an event with mass casualties to confirm the guru's apocalyptic prophesies. Japanese authorities were slow to admit to the threat posed by Aum, partly because of long-standing police reticence to engage in investigations that could be seen as persecution of a religious group. After Aum's 1995 sarin attack on the Tokyo subway, the Japanese government stripped it of its religious-organization status and seized its assets; the government also placed several key cult members, including Asahara, on trial. Residual elements of Aum continue to exist, although the organization's name has been changed to Aleph.

Selected High-Profile Incidents

1993   Unsuccessful attempts to manufacture and release anthrax around Tokyo
1994   Release of sarin in a residential neighborhood in Matsumoto, Japan
1995   Release of sarin on the Tokyo subway system

Hizballah

Hizballah is a militant Islamic organization based in southern Lebanon. It began to operate as a guerrilla organization in 1982, after the Israeli military occupied southern Lebanon in an effort to eliminate incursions into Israel by Palestinian guerrillas using the area as a base of operations. The group's original goal was to compel the Israeli military to withdraw from southern Lebanon. Toward that end, it carried out a series of terrorist attacks, including kidnappings, hijackings, and suicide bombings, and engaged in guerrilla warfare against Western and Israeli targets. Hizballah began as a collection of loosely associated militia groups trained and organized by the Iranian Revolutionary Guards. In 1988, these various groups came under a central command. Throughout its existence, Hizballah has maintained a core fighting force ranging in size from approximately 500 to 4,000 members. Ideologically, it is a Shi'ite organization, placing Iran at the center of its religious and pan-Islamic worldview, but it combines this Islamic orientation with strong Lebanese nationalism. Over the years, Hizballah has benefited from the sponsorship of Iran and Syria, which have provided the group with financial support, training, and arms. Along with guerrilla warfare, Hizballah has mounted various terrorist operations against its adversaries, including hostage-taking, suicide bombings, and Ketusha rocket attacks against civilian targets in northern Israel. In 2000, Hizballah achieved its primary objective when the Israeli military unilaterally withdrew from southern Lebanon. Subsequently, Hizballah has concentrated on transforming itself into a political organization. Members of the group first ran successfully for Parliament in 1992. Hizballah has also continued a low level of attacks against Israel in the Golan Heights and more indirectly through its support of various Palestinian groups fighting the Israelis.

Selected High-Profile Incidents

1980s Abductions of nearly 100 Westerners, including the president of the American University in Beirut, the CIA station chief (who was later killed), and the British special envoy of the Archbishop of Canterbury

1983 Suicide bombings of buildings housing UN peacekeeping forces in Beirut, killing both U.S. Marines and French paratroopers; a subsequent truck bomb attack on the U.S. embassy in Beirut

1985 Hijacking of Trans-World Airlines flight 847, which ended with the execution of a passenger who was in the U.S. Navy

1992 Bombing of the Israeli embassy in Argentina

1996 Suspected involvement in the truck bombing of the Khobar Towers, which housed U.S. military personnel in Saudi Arabia

Jemaah Islamiyah

Jemaah Islamiyah (JI) is a militant Islamist group operating in Southeast Asia. Its goal is to establish separate Islamic communities in the area as a precursor to the creation of a pan-regional Islamic caliphate. JI views *jihad* (holy war) as essential to achieving this vision. JI coalesced in the mid-1990s as an increasingly organized network of individuals who used terrorism and other forms of violence to achieve their goals. It has been closely linked with al Qaeda and operatives involved in *jihad* in Afghanistan. Over its history, the group has had active cells in several different countries, including Indonesia, Malaysia, the Philippines, and Singapore, and has developed a core group of dedicated and well-trained operatives, which likely total several hundred. Its operatives have staged infrequent, but highly effective, bombing attacks in Indonesia and the Philippines and have plans for attacks in Singapore and other Southeast Asian countries. Since 2001, increased counterterrorism operations have resulted in the arrest or killing of many JI personnel, including the group's spiritual leader, Abu Bakar Ba'asyir. Nonetheless, JI, or at least a subgroup of its operatives, has demonstrated a continuing ability to undertake major attacks.

Selected High-Profile Incidents

2000	Bombings of churches across Indonesia on Christmas Eve
2002	Bombing of two nightclubs in Bali
2003	Bombing of the J.W. Marriott Hotel in Jakarta
2004	Bombing of the Australian embassy in Jakarta

The Provisional Irish Republican Army

The goals of the Provisional Irish Republican Army (PIRA) were defined by the long history of the Irish Republican movement. PIRA came into being in 1969, splintering from the rest of the Republican movement because of differences in political and military strategy. Drawing on long-standing Republican traditions that called for violence as the means of pursuing nationalist goals, PIRA defined itself as a military entity. But understanding that it could not directly confront the British armed forces, it utilized terrorism and insurgent violence. PIRA's main targets were the British and the Loyalists of Northern Ireland, who were committed to remaining part of the United Kingdom. Religion defined the nature of the conflict, as Republicans were primarily Catholic and Loyalists were predominantly Protestant. For nearly 30 years, PIRA conducted the vast majority of its operations in Northern Ireland and on the British mainland, with additional attacks or activities in the Irish Republic, continental Europe, and the United States. In 1997, PIRA agreed to a ceasefire as part of the regional peace process and stopped its terrorist operations.

Selected High-Profile Incidents

1979   Assassination of Lord Mountbatten, a relative of Queen Elizabeth II
1993   A large-scale car bombing at Bishopsgate in London's financial district
1994   Mortar attacks on London's Heathrow Airport

The Radical Environmentalist Movement

The Earth Liberation Front (ELF) and the Animal Liberation Front (ALF) are the most prominent terrorist elements, or "fronts," within the radical environmental movement. These groups are dedicated to preventing what they view as the destruction and exploitation of the Earth and its species, both human and non-human. Because of assumed cross-membership of individuals and cross-fertilization among many groups and subunits within the radical environmental movement, law enforcement and counterterrorism efforts frequently treat ELF/ALF and affiliated groups as a single terrorist "organization" for analytical purposes, while recognizing that the groups' diversity adds a unique dynamic. Rejecting the label of "terrorist group," the subgroups instead define themselves as part of a grass-roots social movement. Individually and collectively, these groups lack a formal organizational structure and rely instead on a "leaderless resistance" approach that considers any person who acts on its behalf to be an agent of the group, as long as his or her actions follow the group's guidelines. This sets these movements apart from the other groups examined in this study. During the past three decades, more than 1,000 criminal acts, resulting in more than $100 million in damages, have been committed by radical environmentalists, including ELF/ALF. However, consistent with the disaggregated nature of their activities, no estimate exists of the number of individuals involved. Arson, vandalism, and theft are the ELF/ALF's most frequent actions against property targets belonging to people and businesses that it considers to be engaged in activities harmful to the environment and/or animals.

Selected High-Profile Incidents

1998   Arson of a ski resort in Vail, CO, that caused several million dollars in damage
1999   Arson of the Boise Cascade lumber company
2001   Arson of the Center for Urban Horticulture at the University of Washington, Seattle
2003   Arson and vandalism of 125 sport utility vehicles at auto dealerships and in neighborhoods near Los Angeles

References

Argyris, Chris, and Donald A. Schön, *Organizational Learning: A Theory of Action Perspective*, Reading, MA: Addison-Wesley, 1978.

Arquilla, John, and David Ronfeldt, *Networks and Netwars: The Future of Terror, Crime and Militancy*, Santa Monica, CA: RAND Corporation, 2001.

"Azahari's Tracks," *TEMPO*, September 2, 2003, p. 15.

Baker, John C., "Jemaah Islamiyah," in *Aptitude for Destruction, Volume 2: Case Studies of Organizational Learning in Five Terrorist Groups*, Santa Monica, CA: RAND Corporation, 2005.

Beeby, Mick, and Charles Booth, "Networks and Inter-Organizational Learning: A Critical Review," *The Learning Organization*, Vol. 7, No. 2, 2000, pp. 75–88.

Bell, J. Bowyer, *The Gun in Politics: An Analysis of Irish Political Conflict, 1916–1986*, New Brunswick, NJ: Transaction Books, 1987.

___, *IRA: Tactics and Targets*, Swords, Ireland: Poolberg, 1993.

___, "The Armed Struggle and Underground Intelligence: An Overview," *Studies in Conflict and Terrorism*, Vol. 17, 1994, pp. 115–150.

___, *The Dynamics of the Armed Struggle*, London, UK: Frank Cass, 1998a.

___, *The Secret Army: The IRA*, Dublin, Ireland: Poolbeg, 1998b.

Benjamin, Daniel, and Steven Simon, *The Age of Sacred Terror*, New York: Random House, 2002.

Bohn, Roger E., "Measuring and Managing Technological Knowledge," *Sloan Management Review*, Fall 1994, pp. 61–73.

Byman, Daniel L., Peter Chalk, Bruce Hoffman, William Rosenau, and David Brannan, *Trends in Outside Support for Insurgent Movements*, Santa Monica, CA: RAND Corporation, 2001.

Carley, K., "Organizational Learning and Personnel Turnover," *Organization Science*, Vol. 3, No. 1, 1992, pp. 20–46.

Carley, Kathleen M., Ju-Sung Lee, and David Krackhardt, "Destabilizing Networks," 2001, available at http://www.ksg.harvard.edu/complexity/papers/connections4.pdf (last accessed October 26, 2004).

Chalk, Peter, *Liberation Tigers of Tamil Eelam's (LTTE) International Organization and Operations—A Preliminary Analysis,* Ottawa, Canada: Canadian Security Intelligence Service, 2000.

___, "US Environmental Groups and 'Leaderless Resistance,'" *Jane's Intelligence Review,* July 1, 2001.

Collins, Eamon, and Mick McGovern, *Killing Rage,* London, UK: Granta Books, 1998.

Coogan, Tim Pat, *The IRA: A History,* Niwot, CO: Roberts Rinehart Publishers, 1993.

Cragin, Kim, "Hizballah, The Party of God," in *Aptitude for Destruction, Volume 2: Case Studies of Organizational Learning in Five Terrorist Groups,* Santa Monica, CA: RAND Corporation, 2005.

___, and Sara A. Daly, *The Dynamic Terrorist Threat: An Assessment of Group Motivations and Capabilities in a Changing World,* Santa Monica, CA: RAND Corporation, 2004.

___, and Bruce Hoffman, *Arms Trafficking and Colombia,* Santa Monica, CA: RAND Corporation, 2003.

Crenshaw, Martha, "Innovation: Decision Points in the Trajectory of Terrorism," prepared for the Conference on Trajectories of Terrorist Violence in Europe, Minda de Gunzburg Center for European Studies, Harvard University, Cambridge, MA, March 9–11, 2001.

Cutshaw, Charles Q., "Infantry Weapons: The Way Ahead," *Jane's International Defense Review,* Vol. 52, July 1, 2002, pp. 47–53.

Cyert, Richard M., and James G. March, *A Behavioral Theory of the Firm,* Englewood Cliffs, NJ: Prentice-Hall, 1963.

Davis, Anthony, "Tamil Tiger International," *Jane's Intelligence Review,* Vol. 8, No. 10, October 1, 1996, p. 469.

___, "The Afghan Files: Al Qaeda Documents from Kabul," *Jane's Intelligence Review,* 2002.

Davis, Paul K., and Brian Michael Jenkins, *Deterrence & Influence in Counterterrorism: A Component in the War on al Qaeda,* Santa Monica, CA: RAND Corporation, 2002.

Dodgson, Mark, "Organizational Learning: A Review of Some Literature," *Organizational Studies,* Vol. 14, No. 3, 1993, pp. 375–394.

Dolnik, Adam, and Bhattacharjee, "Hamas: Suicide Bombings, Rockets, or WMD?" *Terrorism and Political Violence,* Vol. 14, No. 3, 2002, pp. 109–128.

Drake, C.J.M., *Terrorists' Target Selection,* New York: St. Martin's Press, 1998.

Easterby-Smith, Mark, Mary Crossan, and Davide Nicolini, "Organizational Learning: Debates Past, Present and Future," *Journal of Management Studies,* Vol. 37, No. 6, 2000, pp. 783–796.

Edmonson, Amy C., Ann B. Winslow, Richard M. J. Bohmer, and Gary P. Pisano, "Learning How and Learning What: Effects of Tacit and Codified Knowledge on Performance Improvement Following Technology Adoption," *Decision Sciences,* Vol. 34, No. 2, 2003, pp. 197–223.

Fiol, C. Marlene, and Marjorie A. Lyles, "Organizational Learning," *Academy of Management Review,* Vol. 10, No. 4, 1985, pp. 803–813.

Foreign and Commonwealth Office: Republic of Ireland Department: Registered Files (WL Series) 1972–1974, *IRA Tactics in Northern Ireland,* British National Archives, FCO 87-1, 1972.

Foreman, Dave, and Bill Haywood, "Ecodefense: A Field Guide to Monkeywrenching," 1989, available at http://www.riseup.net/brady/propaganda/files/Ecodefense_A_Field_Guide_To_Monkeywrenching.txt (last accessed December 9, 2004).

Garvin, David A., "Building a Learning Organization," *Harvard Business Review,* 1993, pp. 78–91.

Geraghty, Tony, *The Irish War: The Hidden Conflict Between the IRA and British Intelligence,* Baltimore, MD: The Johns Hopkins University Press, 2000.

Gertler, Meric S., "Tacit Knowledge and the Economic Geography of Context or The Undefinable Tacitness of Being (There)," Nelson and Winter DRUID Summer Conference, Aalborg, Denmark, June 12–15, 2001.

Gerwehr, Scott, and Russell W. Glenn, *The Art of Darkness: Deception and Urban Operations,* Santa Monica, CA: RAND Corporation, 2000.

___, *Unweaving the Web: Deception and Adaptation in Future Urban Operations,* Santa Monica, CA: RAND Corporation, 2003.

Glover, J. M., *"Northern Ireland Terrorist Trends,"* London: Ministry of Defence, British Government, 1978.

Gopalakrishnan, Shanti, and Paul Bierly, "Analyzing Innovation Adoption Using a Knowledge-Based Approach," *Journal of Engineering and Technology Management,* Vol. 18, 2001, pp. 107–130.

Gunaratna, Rohan, *International and Regional Implications of the Sri Lankan Tamil Insurgency,* Colombo, Sri Lanka: Bandaranaike Centre for International Studies, 1997.

___, "Intelligence Failures Exposed by Tamil Tiger Airport Attack," *Jane's Intelligence Review,* September 2001a, pp. 16–17.

___, "Maritime Terrorism: Future Threats and Responses," International Research Group on Political Violence (IRGPV), United States Institute of Peace (USIP), Washington, DC, April 15, 2001b.

___, *Inside Al Qaeda: Global Network of Terror,* New York: Columbia University Press, 2002.

Hall, Bronwyn H., and Beethika Khan, *Adoption of New Technology,* Cambridge, MA: National Bureau of Economic Research, 2003.

Hardy, Cynthia, Nelson Phillips, and Thomas B. Lawrence, "Resources, Knowledge and Influence: The Organizational Effects of Interorganizational Collaboration," *Journal of Management Studies,* Vol. 40, No. 2, 2003, pp. 321–347.

Harnden, Toby, *Bandit Country: The IRA and South Armagh,* London, UK: Coronet Books, LIR, 2000.

Hedberg, Bo, "How Organizations Learn and Unlearn?" in Paul C. Nyström and William H. Starbuck (eds.), *Handbook of Organizational Design,* Oxford, UK: Oxford University Press, 1981, pp. 3–27.

Hendley, Scott E., and Steve Wegelian, *Report to Congress on the Extent and Effects of Domestic and International Terrorism on Animal Enterprises,* Washington, DC: U.S. Department of Justice and U.S. Department of Agriculture, 1993.

Hirshberg, Peter, "Getting Smart," *Jerusalem Post,* December 17, 1992.

Hoffman, Bruce, *Inside Terrorism,* New York: Columbia University Press, 1998.

___, "Change and Continuity in Terrorism," *Studies in Conflict and Terrorism,* Vol. 24, 2001, pp. 417–428.

Holden, R., "The Contagiousness of Aircraft Hijacking," *American Journal of Sociology,* Vol. 91, 1986, pp. 874–904.

Hong, Jacky, "Structuring for Organizational Learning," *The Learning Organization,* Vol. 6, No. 4, 1999, pp. 173–185.

Huber, George P., "Organizational Learning: The Contributing Process and the Literatures," *Organization Science,* Vol. 2, No. 1, 1991, pp. 88–115.

International Crisis Group (ICG), *Indonesia Backgrounder: How the Jemaah Islamiyah Terrorist Network Operates,* 2003.

Jackson, Brian A., "Technology Acquisition by Terrorist Groups: Threat Assessment Informed by Lessons from Private Sector Technology Adoption," *Studies in Conflict and Terrorism,* Vol. 24, 2001, pp. 183–213.

___, "The Provisional Irish Republican Army," in *Aptitude for Destruction, Volume 2: Case Studies of Organizational Learning in Five Terrorist Groups,* Santa Monica, CA: RAND Corporation, 2005.

Jenkins, Brian Michael, *Countering Al Qaeda: An Appreciation of the Situation and Suggestions for Strategy,* Santa Monica, CA: RAND Corporation, 2002.

Jones, K. K., "Competing to Learn in Japan," *McKinsey Quarterly,* Vol. 1, 1991, pp. 45–57.

Kaplan, David E., and Andrew Marshall, *The Cult at the End of the World,* New York: Crown Publishers, 1996.

Kaplan, Jeffery, "Right Wing Violence in North America," in Tore Bjørgo (ed.), *Terror from the Extreme Right,* London, UK: Frank Cass, 1995, pp. 44–95.

Kenney, Michael, "The Challenge of Eradicating Transnational Criminal Networks: Lessons from the War on Drugs," paper presented at the 2002 Annual Meeting of the American Political Science Association, Boston, MA, August 29–September 1, 2002.

___, "From Pablo to Osama: Counter-terrorism Lessons from the War on Drugs," *Survival,* Vol. 45, No. 3, 2003a, pp. 187–206.

___, "Intelligence Games: Comparing the Intelligence Capabilities of Law Enforcement Agencies and Drug Trafficking Enterprises," *International Journal of Intelligence and CounterIntelligence,* Vol. 16, 2003b, pp. 212–243.

Kim, D. H., "The Link Between Individual and Organizational Learning," *Sloan Management Review,* Fall 1993, pp. 37–50.

Kitfield, James, "Osama's Learning Curve," *National Journal,* Vol. 33, No. 45, 2001, pp. 3506–3511.

Leader, Stefan H., and Peter Probst, "The Earth Liberation Front and Environmental Terrorism," *Terrorism and Political Violence,* Vol. 15, No. 4, 2003, pp. 37–58.

Leitenberg, Milton, "Aum Shinrikyo's Efforts to Produce Biological Weapons: A Case Study in the Serial Propagation of Misinformation," *Terrorism and Political Violence,* Vol. 11, No. 4, 1999, pp. 149–158.

Libicki, Martin C., and Shari Lawrence Pfleeger, *Collecting the Dots: Problem Formulation and Solution Elements,* Santa Monica, CA: RAND Corporation, 2004.

Lipshitz, Raanan, Micha Popper, and Victor J. Friedman, "A Multifacet Model of Organizational Learning," *The Journal of Applied Behavioral Science,* Vol. 38, No. 1, 2002, pp. 78–98.

Long, James, and Bryan Denson, "Can Sabotage Have a Place in a Democratic Community?" *The Oregonian,* September 29, 1999.

Lutes, Chuck, "Al-Qaida in Action and Learning: A Systems Approach," 2001, available at http://www.au.af.mil/au/awc/awcgate/readings/al_qaida2.htm (last accessed October 21, 2004).

MacDermott, Diarmaid, "Three Get 20 Years on Bomb Factory Charges," *Irish News,* February 1, 1998, available at http://archives.tcm.ie/irishexaminer/1998/02/14/ihead.htm.

McAllister, Brad, "Al Qaeda and the Innovative Firm: Demythologizing the Network," *Studies in Conflict and Terrorism,* Vol. 27, 2004, pp. 297–319.

McCauley, Clark, "Psychological Issues in Understanding Terrorism and the Response to Terrorism," in Christopher E. Stout (ed.), *The Psychology of Terrorism,* Westport, CT: Greenwood Publishing Group, 2002.

McCormick, Gordon H., "Terrorist Decision Making," *Annual Review of Political Science,* Vol. 6, 2003, pp. 473–507.

McGill, Michael E., and John W. Slocum, Jr., "Unlearning the Organization," *Organizational Dynamics,* Vol. 22, No. 2, 1993, pp. 67–79.

Merari, Ariel, "Terrorism as a Strategy of Insurgency," *Terrorism and Political Violence,* Vol. 5, No. 4, 1993, pp. 213–251.

Miller, D., "A Preliminary Topology of Organizational Learning: Synthesizing the Literature," *Journal of Management,* Vol. 22, No. 3, 1996, pp. 485–505.

Moghadam, Assaf, "Palestinian Suicide Terrorism in the Second Intifada: Motivations and Organizational Aspects," *Studies in Conflict and Terrorism*, Vol. 26, 2003, pp. 65–92.

Mowery, David C., Joanne B. Oxley, and Brian S. Silverman, "Strategic Alliances and Inter-firm Knowledge Transfer," *Strategic Management Journal*, Vol. 17, 1996, pp. 77–91.

O'Callaghan, Sean, *The Informer*, London, UK: Corgi Books, 1999.

O'Doherty, Shane, *The Volunteer: A Former IRA Man's True Story*, London, UK: Fount, 1993.

Olcott, Martha Brill, and Bakhtiyar Babajanov, "The Terrorist Notebooks," *Foreign Policy*, March–April, 2003, pp. 30–40.

Ortiz, Roman D., "Insurgent Strategies in the Post–Cold War: The Case of the Revolutionary Armed Forces of Colombia," *Studies in Conflict and Terrorism*, Vol. 25, 2002, pp. 127–143.

Overgaard, Per Baltzer, "The Scale of Terrorist Attacks as a Signal of Resources," *Journal of Conflict Resolution*, Vol. 38, No. 3, 1994, pp. 452–478.

Parachini, John, "Putting WMD Terrorism into Perspective," *The Washington Quarterly*, Vol. 26, No. 4, 2003, pp. 37–50.

___, "Aum Shinrikyo," in *Aptitude for Destruction, Volume 2: Case Studies of Organizational Learning in Five Terrorist Groups*, Santa Monica, CA: RAND Corporation, 2005.

Pate-Cornell, Elisabeth, and Seth Guikema, "Probabilistic Modeling of Terrorist Threats: A Systems Analysis Approach to Setting Priorities Among Countermeasures," *Military Operations Research*, Vol. 7, No. 4, 2002, pp. 5–20.

Peci, Patrizio, *Io L'infame (Trans: I, The Contemptible One)*, as told to Giordano Brunok Guerri and Arnoldo Mondadori Editore S.p.A Milano, 1983 (Foreign Broadcast Information Service Translation, March 20, 1985, JPRS-TOT-85-016).

Pluchinsky, Dennis A., "Western Europe's Red Terrorists: The Fighting Communist Organizations," in Yonah Alexander and Dennis A. Pluchinsky (eds.), *Europe's Red Terrorists: The Fighting Communist Organizations*, Portland, OR: Frank Cass, 1992, pp. 16–54.

Ranstorp, Magnus, *Hizb'allah in Lebanon: The Politics of the Western Hostage Crisis*, New York: St. Martin's Press, 1997.

Ressa, Maria, *Seeds of Terror: An Eyewitness Account of Al-Qaeda's Newest Center of Operations in Southeast Asia*, New York: Free Press, 2003.

Robinson, David F., Grant T. Savage, and Kim Sydow Campbell, "Organizational Learning, Diffusion of Innovation, and International Collaboration in Telemedicine," *Health Care Management Review*, Vol. 28, No. 1, 2003, pp. 68–78.

Romme, Georges, and Ron Dillen, "Mapping the Landscape of Organizational Learning," *European Management Journal*, Vol. 15, No. 1, 1997, pp. 68–78.

Rosenau, William, "Aum Shinrikyo's Biological Weapons Program: Why Did It Fail?" *Studies in Conflict and Terrorism*, Vol. 24, 2001, pp. 289–301.

Sandler, Todd, and Daniel G. Arce M., "Terrorism & Game Theory," *Simulation & Gaming,* Vol. 34, No. 3, 2003, pp. 319–337.

Schwarzen, Christopher, "Environmental Radicals Shift Targets to Streets," *Seattle Times,* June 12, 2004, available at http://seattletimes.nwsource.com/html/snohomishcountynews/2001954671_elf11m.html.

Shrivastava, Paul, "A Typology of Organizational Learning Systems," *Journal of Management Studies,* Vol. 20, No. 1, 1983, pp. 7–28.

Simmons, Jeremy, et al., *Closing the Gaps: A Strategy for Gaining the Initiative in the War on Terror,* Monterey, CA: Center on Terrorism & Irregular Warfare, Naval Postgraduate School, 2003.

Smithson, Amy E., *Ataxia: The Chemical and Biological Terrorism Threat and the U.S. Response,* Washington, DC: The Henry L. Stimson Center, 1999.

Stern, Jessica, "The Protean Enemy," *Foreign Affairs,* Vol. 82, No. 4, 2003, pp. 27–40.

Steven, Graeme C.S., and Rohan Gunaratna, *Counterterrorism: A Reference Handbook*, Santa Barbara, CA: ABC-CLIO, 2004.

Susser, Leslie, "Hizballah Masters the TOW," *The Jerusalem Report*, March 13, 2000.

Takeyh, Ray, and Nikolas Gvosdev, "Do Terrorist Networks Need a Home?" *The Washington Quarterly,* Vol. 25, No. 3, 2002, pp. 97–108.

Taudes, Alfred, Michael Trcka, and Martin Lukanowicz, "Organizational Learning in Production Networks," *Journal of Economic Behavior & Organization,* Vol. 47, 2002, pp. 141–163.

Thomas, Troy S., and William D. Casebeer, *Violent Systems: Defeating Terrorists, Insurgents, and Other Non-State Adversaries,* Colorado Springs, CO: United States Air Force Academy, United States Air Force Institute for National Security Studies, 2004.

Trujillo, Horacio R., "The Radical Environmental Movement," in *Aptitude for Destruction, Volume 2: Case Studies of Organizational Learning in Five Terrorist Groups,* Santa Monica, CA: RAND Corporation, 2005.

___, and Brian A. Jackson, "Organizational Learning and Terrorist Groups," in James J.F. Forest (ed.), *Teaching Terror: Knowledge Transfer in the Terrorist World,* forthcoming.

Tucker, David, "Combating the Terrorist Threat," in James M. Smith and William C. Thomas (eds.), *The Terrorism Threat and U.S. Government Response: Operational and Organizational Factors,* Colorado Springs, CO: United States Air Force Academy, United States Air Force Institute for National Security Studies, 2001, pp. 129–154.

Turnbull, Wayne, "A Tangled Web of Southeast Asian Islamic Terrorism: The Jemaah Islamiyah Terrorist Network," 2003, available at http://www.terrorismcentral.com/Library/terroristgroups/JemaahIslamiyah/JITerror/JIContents.html (last accessed July 6, 2004).

Urban, Mark, *Big Boys' Rules: The Secret Struggle Against the IRA,* London, UK: Faber & Faber, 1992.

Wang, Catherine L., and Pervaiz K. Ahmed, "Organisational Learning: A Critical Review," *The Learning Organization,* Vol. 10, No. 1, 2003, pp. 8–17.

White Paper: The Jemaah Islamiyah Arrests and the Threat of Terrorism, Republic of Singapore: Ministry of Home Affairs, 2003.

Willems, Helmut, "Development, Patterns and Causes of Violence Against Foreigners in Germany: Social and Biographical Characteristics of Perpetrators and the Process of Escalation," in Tore Bjørgo (ed.), *Terror from the Extreme Right,* London, UK: Frank Cass, 1995, pp. 44–95.

Zollo, Maurizio, and Sidney G. Winter, "Deliberate Learning and the Evolution of Dynamic Capabilities," *Organization Science,* Vol. 13, No. 3, 2002, pp. 339–351.